Early Praise for *Intuitive Python*

Intuitive Python: Productive Development for Projects That Last is ideally written for the programmer who has learned just enough Python to be dangerous. David Muller's concise collection of Python best practices will keep such programmers from making rookie mistakes while learning about a collection of the best practices that the Python community has to offer.

➤ **Mike Riley**
   President, Ingenious Solutions

Intuitive Python: Productive Development for Projects That Last is an excellent on-ramp to writing Python like a professional. The practices and tools introduced in this book are sure to improve the quality of any project incorporating them.

➤ **Riley Yeakle**
   Data Engineer, Guidebook, Inc.

This short book shows practical examples and best practices that take most programmers years to learn.

➤ **Miki Tebeka**
   CEO, 353solutions

I wish I had this book at the beginning of my career. It helps you to understand Python and its ecosystem smoothly and efficiently.

➤ **Estera Kot**
   Senior Cloud Solution Architect, Microsoft

Intuitive Python

Productive Development for Projects that Last

David Muller

The Pragmatic Bookshelf

Raleigh, North Carolina

Many of the designations used by manufacturers and sellers to distinguish their products are claimed as trademarks. Where those designations appear in this book, and The Pragmatic Programmers, LLC was aware of a trademark claim, the designations have been printed in initial capital letters or in all capitals. The Pragmatic Starter Kit, The Pragmatic Programmer, Pragmatic Programming, Pragmatic Bookshelf, PragProg and the linking *g* device are trademarks of The Pragmatic Programmers, LLC.

Every precaution was taken in the preparation of this book. However, the publisher assumes no responsibility for errors or omissions, or for damages that may result from the use of information (including program listings) contained herein.

For our complete catalog of hands-on, practical, and Pragmatic content for software developers, please visit *https://pragprog.com*.

The team that produced this book includes:

CEO: Dave Rankin
COO: Janet Furlow
Managing Editor: Tammy Coron
Development Editor: Adaobi Obi Tulton
Copy Editor: Karen Galle
Layout: Gilson Graphics
Founders: Andy Hunt and Dave Thomas

For sales, volume licensing, and support, please contact *support@pragprog.com*.

For international rights, please contact *rights@pragprog.com*.

ISBN-13: 978-1-68050-823-9
Book version: P1.0—June 2021

Contents

Acknowledgments

Many people came together to make this book possible. I especially want to thank my editor, Adaobi Obi Tulton. Adaobi worked with me every step of the way to produce this book—she provided expert guidance, advice, and inline feedback as the book evolved and took form.

A number of other individuals also read drafts of this book and contributed valuable comments and changes:

- Riley Yeakle
- Thomas Genin
- Benjamin Muskalla
- Adam Gladstone
- Anuja Kelkar
- Estera Kot
- Mike Riley
- Andy Lester
- Miki Tebeka
- Tim Ottinger
- Michael Swaine

Preface

Developers build applications in Python because it emphasizes readability, low barrier to entry, and an expansive ecosystem of open source tooling. All kinds of developers—scientists, researchers, professional software engineers, and even beginners—embrace these benefits and choose Python to power their projects.

Python's long history and high level of adoption mean you have access to a large suite of third-party tools in addition to Python's expansive batteries-included standard library. Managing Python projects requires knowledge of the tools available to you and adopting patterns that will help your Python code stand the test of time.

In this book, you will learn about some of Python's greatest strengths, weaknesses, and tools to maximize the utility and resiliency of your Python projects.

Who This Book Is For

This book contains content for programmers—especially programmers newer to Python—interested in leveling up the projects they maintain with Python.

Rather than spend time on Python syntax and control flow, we'll focus on tools, patterns, and knowledge to help you build an intuition for working with Python.

As you might expect, this book can't and won't cover everything you need to know about Python. Instead, it tries to give you access to high-impact tools and knowledge that can improve your skills and make you feel comfortable with some of Python's capabilities and boundaries. The contents of this book expose you to important parts of Python that will make the language more pleasant and useful to you.

What's Inside

The chapters in this book start with a broad focus that grows increasingly specific as you build a more nuanced understanding of Python:

- You'll start in Chapter 1, Diving into Life with Python, on page 1 by running code in Python's interactive console, debugging it using Python's built-in debugger, and automatically eliminating classes of bugs before you run code with static analysis tools, including mypy.

- Next in Chapter 2, Shifting Up with the Standard Library, on page 33, you'll use some of the most powerful and practical parts of Python's standard library. Profile your procedures with Python's built-in profiler, execute external programs with Python's high-level subprocess harness, and write concise code using the collections module.

- With some of the best parts of the standard library under your belt, you'll experiment with Python's concurrency model in Chapter 3, Ramping Up with Concurrent Code, on page 67. You'll develop patterns for using Python's thread and process abstractions to their full potential, even under the constraints imposed by Python's infamous GIL (global interpreter lock).

- In Chapter 4, Avoiding Traps, on page 87, you build on your standard library knowledge and sharpen your Python instincts so you avoid all manner of potential pitfalls. Dodge the mutable default argument trap, keep track of time, and serialize your data reliably.

- As the book closes out in Chapter 5, Standing Guard When Python Breaks Free, on page 103, you'll train your eye to keep watch on emergent problems. Prevent unexpected variable clobbering and unintended access. Download and run third-party packages, and do so safely without compromising on security. Wrap up with newfound intuition for harnessing and hardening your code.

Whether you're a new or experienced programmer, this book gives you an understanding of Python that will help hone your Python instincts and make your projects more successful.

Using the Code in This Book

To run the code in this book, you will need Python 3.7 or newer. The most convenient way to run this book's code is to use the companion Docker image which contains an appropriate Python version and all the source code pre-downloaded.[1] We'll cover options for running this book's code in more detail in the next section.

All of the source code in this book (and any errata) can also be downloaded from this book's web page.[2] Additionally, if you've purchased the ebook, clicking the little gray box above any code extract directly downloads the extract for you.

Let's get started!

---

1. https://github.com/DavidMuller/intuitive-python-book
2. https://pragprog.com/titles/dmpython

## CHAPTER 1

Diving into Life with Python

Eric could not stop laughing. We'd only just begun watching *Monty Python and the Holy Grail* and he was in stitches. Pretty soon the movie started catching me too, and I couldn't help but laugh. For days afterward, we repeated our favorite gags—questioning each other about the airspeed velocity of unladen swallows and constantly yelling, "it's just a flesh wound!"

In case you haven't seen *Monty Python and the Holy Grail*, it's a 1975 film by a surreal comedy troupe called Monty Python. Suffice to say, their movie *Monty Python and the Holy Grail* is absurd. Eric and I were only maybe eight or nine years old when we first saw it, which probably made the movie all the more hilarious to us.

Fast forward ten years later. I was in college learning to program, first with C, and then C++, and occasionally Java sprinkled in. For me, it was pretty much the opposite of laughing. I remember the torture of forgetting null terminators for C strings and never being able to exit vim (my text editor) cleanly.

After about two years programming in the dark, my friend Riley introduced me to programming in Python. I remember laughing not only at how easily I could write the programs I wanted to, but also at how easily I could read them back to myself later. Programming in Python wasn't quite the same joy as watching *Monty Python and the Holy Grail* for the first time, but the thrill of finding a language that felt so natural was joyful.

Guido van Rossum (Python's inventor) named his programming language after the Monty Python comedy troupe. I don't know exactly why Guido named his language after the group, but just as Monty Python has had an enduring influence on comedy, Python has enjoyed tremendous popularity and staying power in its 30+ years of existence. And like Monty Python, the Python programming language—in all the years I've used it—has kept programming enjoyable and on the lighter side. In this book, you'll explore how Python can feel this way for you too.

To run the Python code in this book, you'll use Python version 3.7 or higher. In the first part of this chapter, you'll see how to launch a Python interactive console (or download Python if you don't yet have it).

After you launch Python's interactive console to run programs, you'll debug them using Python's built-in debugger and run static analysis tools to check your code for errors before you run it. Let's get started.

Setting Up Your Environment and Using This Book's Companion Docker Image

First, let's set up your machine so you are able to run Python. Here are a few different approaches you can take:

1. ✪ Run Python using this book's companion Docker image (recommended):[1]
   - Install Docker.[2]

   - Execute docker run --pull=always --interactive --tty --rm ghcr.io/davidmuller/intuitive-python-book/intuitive-python-book:latest /bin/bash

   - You are now logged into an ephemeral container with an appropriate version of Python and all this book's source code downloaded into the current working directory.

   - If you are reading a paper version of this book or using a digital reader that makes copy/pasting the preceding docker run command difficult, visit the homepage of this book's companion Docker image for an easier copy/pasting medium.[3]

2. Run Python on macOS or Linux:
   - Type python3 --version to see if you have Python 3.7 or newer, else download one.[4]

3. Run Python on Windows:
   - Type python3 --version to see if you have Python 3.7 or newer, else download one.[5]

---

1. https://github.com/DavidMuller/intuitive-python-book
2. https://docs.docker.com/get-docker/
3. https://github.com/DavidMuller/intuitive-python-book
4. https://www.python.org/downloads/
5. https://www.python.org/downloads/

- ⚠ Warning: the examples in this book work best when run using options 1 or 2. For the smoothest experience, I recommend those options so you can avoid small differences that appear when you run some examples on Windows.

You can download the raw source code for all printed examples from this book's web page.[6] If you're using the companion Docker image and would like to know more about Docker, we'll cover some additional details in Try Out Different Versions of Python with Docker, on page 11.

Now that you're setup to run Python, let's dive in.

Using Python's Interactive Console to Run Programs

Python provides an interactive console where you can run Python code dynamically (without, for example, creating any source code files beforehand). Start Python's interactive console by running python3 from your command line:

```
$ python3
Python 3.9.2 (default, Mar 12 2021, 18:54:15)
[GCC 8.3.0] on linux
Type "help", "copyright", "credits", or "license" for more information.
>>>
```

After you run python3, you'll see several lines describing the version of Python you're running. In the preceding example, Python is on version 3.9.2. As a reminder, the examples in this book all require Python 3.7 or higher.

After running python3, your cursor will be placed just after the >>> characters. This is where you can type and run Python code. (The >>> characters just serve as your prompt and are not syntactically or otherwise important in any way.) Let's start by outputting the text hello world:

```
>>> print("hello world")
hello world
>>>
```

Calling Python's built-in print function outputs the "hello world" string to stdout, and indeed, you should see that text outputted on your machine in between two >>> entries.

The Python interactive console allows you to run any valid Python code, and this includes assigning variables. In this next example, you assign a list of strings to a variable named animals:

---

6. https://pragprog.com/titles/dmpython

```
>>> animals = ["cat", "dog", "fox"]
>>> print(animals)
['cat', 'dog', 'fox']
>>>
```

The animals variable is assigned to a list containing three strings. Calling print on that list outputs a representation of that list to stdout.

You can also import and use other modules from inside the Python interactive console. Let's try an example where you import the datetime standard library module:

```
>>> import datetime
>>> eight_twelve = datetime.time(hour=8, minute=12)
>>> print(eight_twelve)
08:12:00
>>> eight_twelve
datetime.time(8, 12)
>>>
```

import datetime makes the datetime standard library module available to subsequent lines of Python. datetime.time is a class that can be used to represent a point in time of a 24-hour day. When you call datetime.time(hour=8, minute=12), it constructs a datetime.time object representing 8:12 a.m. and 0 seconds. That object is then bound to the variable named eight_twelve. Calling print eight_twelve, yields a string representation of eight_twelve 08:12:00.

Notably, just typing eight_twelve and hitting Enter was also enough for the interactive console to output information about eight_twelve (even though you did not call the print function). Whenever you evaluate a Python expression in the interactive console by typing it and then pressing Enter, Python prints the repr of that expression.[7]

You can think of the repr as an expression's debugging representation—a text representation meant to help you understand more about the expression. In this case, the repr of eight_twelve helps you understand that eight_twelve is assigned to a datetime.time object. Calling print(eight_twelve), by contrast, only outputs 08:12:00—a useful string, but one that doesn't reveal much about the underlying object pointed to by the eight_twelve variable.

repr is actually a built-in Python function, so you can call the repr function at any time to produce helpful debugging information:

---

7. https://docs.python.org/3/library/functions.html?#repr

```
>>> import datetime
>>> eight_twelve = datetime.time(hour=8, minute=12)
>>> eight_twelve
datetime.time(8, 12)
>>> repr(eight_twelve)
'datetime.time(8, 12)'
>>> print(repr(eight_twelve))
datetime.time(8, 12)
>>>
```

Just evaluating eight_twelve outputs the repr representation of eight_twelve that indicates it's a datetime.time object. Actually calling the built-in repr function itself on eight_twelve returns a string. Calling print on repr(eight_twelve) outputs text identical to just typing eight_twelve and hitting Enter. So, you can think of just eight_twelve (or any other expression) as shorthand for saying print(repr(eight_twelve)). It is often very useful to just find an object or expression and hit Enter so you can learn more about it.

How Can I Define a Custom repr?

 To define a repr on your own class, you implement a method on your class with the following signature def __repr__(self).[8] Your __repr__ method should return a string: that's the string that will be printed when developers ask for debug representations in the console or using the repr built-in function.

Adding Code to the Interactive Console

The Python interactive console also allows you to input Python code that spans more than one line. You can, for example, type (or paste) function and class definitions into the console to make them available for your use. As an example, let's say you wrote a function that adds two numbers and wanted to try it out in the console:

```
def add(a, b):
    return a + b
```

You can paste this code directly into the interactive console to make it available to your program:

```
>>> def add(a, b):
...     return a + b
...
>>>
```

8. https://docs.python.org/3/reference/datamodel.html#object.__repr__

Once you've pasted in the add function, you could then use it in subsequent lines of the interactive console:

```
>>> add(1, 2)
3
>>> add(3, 4)
7
>>>
```

Calling the add function on 1 and 2 yields 3, and adding 3 with 4 yields 7. Pasting snippets of code into the interactive console can be a great way to try out new Python you are writing or trying to debug.

Better Text Editing with Alternative Interactive Consoles

Python's built-in interactive console is an excellent tool, but there are also third-party interactive consoles available that are a little more advanced. ipython, in particular, is an alternative interactive console with powerful Tab autocompletion features and more forgiving support for editing code blocks that you paste or type into the console.[9]

Inspecting Unfamiliar Objects

The Python interactive console (especially when combined with a third-party console like ipython) is a great sandbox workspace for you to explore and try out code interactively.[10] When you are running code adhoc in the interactive console, it can be helpful to inspect objects to see how you can use them. There are many tools, for doing this, but four of the most useful are help, _doc_, dir, and _mro_. Let's consider each in turn.

Using help to Inspect Objects

You can use the built-in function help to get verbose output describing a function, class, or object:

```
>>> help(print)
Help on built-in function print in module builtins:

print(...)
    print(value, ..., sep=' ', end='\n', file=sys.stdout, flush=False)

    Prints the values to a stream, or to sys.stdout by default.
    Optional keyword arguments:
    file:  a file-like object (stream); defaults to the current sys.stdout.
    sep:   string inserted between values, default a space.
```

9.   https://pypi.org/project/ipython/
10. https://pypi.org/project/ipython/

```
    end:    string appended after the last value, default a newline.
    flush: whether to forcibly flush the stream.
>>>
```

In the preceding example, you call the help function with the print function as its argument. help outputs information about the print function: what arguments print accepts and some documentation about those arguments.

You can call help with just about any object. For example, you can even call help on the lower instance method of a string object:

```
>>> some_string = "ABC"
>>> help(some_string.lower)
Help on built-in function lower:

lower() method of builtins.str instance
    Return a copy of the string converted to lowercase.

>>> some_string.lower()
'abc'
>>>
```

Calling help(some_string.lower) provides information about the lower function available on string objects (which lowercases strings like "ABC" to "abc"). Whenever you are working with an unfamiliar object or module, it can always help to run help on it to give you some high-level information.

Using __doc__ to Retrieve Docstrings

help provides useful output, but sometimes its output can be quite long. Occasionally, it is enough to just look at the docstring of a particular function or class for more details. The __doc__ attribute allows you to view the docstring of the object in question:

```
>>> def is_even(number):
...     """This function returns True if number is even, False otherwise"""
...     return number % 2 == 0
...
>>> is_even.__doc__
'This function returns True if number is even, False otherwise'
>>>
```

In the preceding example, you define a function named is_even that has a docstring (in between the triple quotes) Retrieving the __doc__ attribute on the is_even function returns the docstring of is_even. Helpfully, the docstring explains what the is_even function does and what values a caller can see returned by the function.

What Is a Docstring?

 Docstrings are string literals that occur as the first statement of a function, class, or module (for example, the first statement in the is_even function in the example is its docstring).[11] Python programmers use these strings to document the behaviors of code for other developers. You'll usually see these strings defined between triple quotes like """Example docstring""".

Docstrings in the standard library and well-maintained third-party packages frequently are filled out with useful information. For example, datetime.time provides a succinct and helpful docstring:

```
>>> import datetime
>>> print(datetime.time.__doc__)
time([hour[, minute[, second[, microsecond[, tzinfo]]]]]) --> a time object

All arguments are optional. tzinfo may be None, or an instance of
a tzinfo subclass. The remaining arguments may be ints.

>>>
```

The docstring of datetime.time describes what arguments datetime.time accepts and what data types those arguments are expected to be. You could certainly have called help(datetime.time) to retrieve some of the same information, but the __doc__ shortcut is convenient and often returns slightly less output.

Note that __doc__ will return None if the underlying object itself doesn't have a docstring:

```
>>> def example_fcn():
...     return 2
...
>>> print(example_fcn.__doc__)
None
>>>
```

The example_fcn function doesn't have a docstring, so running example_fcn.__doc__ just returns None.

Now that we've seen how to interactively gather documentation about a function using help and __doc__, let's use the built-in function dir to list all available attributes and methods on an object.

---

11. https://www.python.org/dev/peps/pep-0257/

Discovering Attributes and Methods with dir

Sometimes you'll be working with an object and will want to quickly find all the attributes and methods you can call on that object. The built-in function dir allows you to find these:

```
>>> some_list = []
>>> dir(some_list)
['__add__', '__class__', '__contains__', '__delattr__', '__delitem__',
 '__dir__', '__doc__', '__eq__', '__format__', '__ge__', '__getattribute__',
 '__getitem__', '__gt__', '__hash__', '__iadd__', '__imul__', '__init__',
 '__init_subclass__', '__iter__', '__le__', '__len__', '__lt__', '__mul__',
 '__ne__', '__new__', '__reduce__', '__reduce_ex__', '__repr__',
 '__reversed__', '__rmul__', '__setattr__', '__setitem__', '__sizeof__',
 '__str__', '__subclasshook__', 'append', 'clear', 'copy', 'count', 'extend',
 'index', 'insert', 'pop', 'remove', 'reverse', 'sort']
>>>
```

Calling dir on some_list reveals all the attributes and methods available on the underlying list object. If you exclude the underscore prefixed attributes and methods, you see append, clear, copy, count, and so on as available methods to call on some_list. These methods are provided by the Python standard library.[12] You can now try using help or __doc__ on these individual methods to learn more about each of them.

If underscore-prefixed methods are private, then why can we call __doc__ and __mro__ (covered next)? We'll discuss privacy more in Maintaining Privacy in a Public World, on page 112, but for now its enough to know that __doc__ and __mro__ are innocent enough (and not truly private): they are safe to call at any time.

Enumerating Class Hierarchies With *mro* (Method Resolution Order)

The last inspection tool we'll explore is the __mro__ attribute. __mro__ allows you to look at a class's hierarchy. For example, you can inspect the class hierarchy of the built-in Exception class:

```
>>> Exception.__mro__
(<class 'Exception'>, <class 'BaseException'>, <class 'object'>)
>>>
```

__mro__ stands for, "method resolution order." So, in the preceding example, you learn that when you try to access an attribute or call a method on the Exception class, it will first look in the Exception class for that attribute or method. If nothing is found on Exception, then a lookup will be performed on the BaseException class. Finally, a lookup will be performed on the object class if nothing

---

12. https://docs.python.org/3/tutorial/datastructures.html#more-on-lists

was found in BaseException or Exception. In terms of hierarchy: Exception descends from BaseException, which descends from object. (Note that all Python classes end their inheritance tree with class object.)

__mro__ is particularly helpful for investigating multiple inheritance. For example, you can use __mro__ to understand a class hierarchy when one class simultaneously inherits from multiple classes:

```
>>> class A:
...     pass  # `pass` is a do-nothing placeholder "no operation" statement
...
>>> class X(A):
...     pass
...
>>> class Y(A):
...     pass
...
>>> class Z(X, Y):
...     pass
...
>>> Z.__mro__
(<class '__main__.Z'>, <class '__main__.X'>, <class '__main__.Y'>,
<class '__main__.A'>, <class 'object'>)
>>>
```

In the preceding example, four classes are defined: A, X, Y, and Z. Both class X and class Y inherit from class A. class Z inherits from both X and Y as denoted by (X, Y). If we were to call some method on class Z, what would be the lookup order? There are three classes in the hierarchy, and—unless you are well-studied in Python inheritance—it's probably not immediately obvious which ones takes precedence over others.

Over time you may come to memorize the inheritance rules, but you should almost always inspect __mro__ to be sure what the order for a given class is. In this case, __mro__ reveals that the resolution order is Z, X, Y, A, and then the default of object. In other words, if a method isn't found on Z, then class X is checked first for a match, followed by Y, then A, and finally object.

Should I Use help, __doc__, dir, and __mro__ at Runtime?

 No. help, __doc__, dir, and __mro__ all improve your ability to debug interactively. None of these methods, however, are intended to be used at runtime. If—for some reason—you need to dynamically inspect an object's docstring, function signature, or the like, you can use the inspect standard library module.[13]

---

13. https://docs.python.org/3/library/inspect.html

You're off to a quick start: you've launched Python, explored the interactive console, and inspected objects that you encountered along the way. In the next section, you'll learn how you can easily try out entirely different versions of the Python interpreter.

Try Out Different Versions of Python with Docker

The maintainers of Python regularly release improved versions of the language. New versions of Python frequently contain new modules and performance improvements. One of the easiest ways to try out these new Python versions is with Docker.

You may already be familiar with Docker, or have just tried it out by using this book's companion image introduced in Setting Up Your Environment and Using This Book's Companion Docker Image, on page 2.

In case you aren't familiar: Docker is a virtualization technology that lets you bundle code and packages together in an image and run them in something called a container. Docker images are static bundles of code and packages, and Docker containers are the running version of an image. For the purposes of this section, you can think of Docker containers as lightweight and isolated virtual machines that you can start quickly and throw away when you're done with them.

It will be easier to understand the power of Docker if we look at two brief examples using official Docker images published by the Python language maintainers.[14]

If you'd like to run these examples along on your computer, first install Docker by downloading it from the Docker website.[15]

After you've installed Docker, you can use it to create a Docker container running Python 3.8.8 by executing the following:

```
docker run --rm --interactive --tty python:3.8.8 /bin/bash
```

If you run the preceding example, you should see a bash shell open up in the Docker container with access to Python 3.8.8:

```
root@751c47625400:/# python3 --version
Python 3.8.8
root@751c47625400:/#
```

The run command instructs docker to create a container running the given image (in our case python:3.8.8). The --rm flag instructs docker to delete the container as it

---

14. https://hub.docker.com/_/python/
15. https://docs.docker.com/get-docker/

exits (recall that containers are generally thought of as disposable and ephemeral). The --interactive and --tty flags instruct docker to create a new terminal and attach it to your stdin so you can interact with the container dynamically. /bin/bash is the command we want to run in the new container. Since we want a shell to play with, running /bin/bash launches a bash shell that we can poke around the container with. As soon as we exit the bash shell, the container also exits and stops running. Think of the container as a temporary workspace.

Running python3 --version in the container reveals that Python is on version 3.8.8. Conveniently, if you tweak the image specified in your docker run command, you can invoke a different version of Python:

```
docker run --rm --interactive --tty python:3.9.2 /bin/bash
```

```
root@0749d6f0b139:/# python3 --version
Python 3.9.2
root@0749d6f0b139:/#
```

The preceding example is identical to the first example, except we've replaced the Docker image python:3.8.8 with python:3.9.2. Now, inside of the container, we have access to a Python 3.9.2 interpreter. The Python team regularly publishes new Python versions and companion Docker containers—so you can easily try out new interpreters in an isolated Docker container at any time. Conveniently, you can always just run docker run --rm --interactive --tty python:3.9.2 python (in other words, replace the /bin/bash command with python) to drop into a temporary Python interactive console running the Python version of your choice.

If you want to go a step farther with the container, you can mount files from your operating system into the Docker container and use them. For example, you can mount an arbitrary directory into a Python 3.8.8 Docker container:

```
docker run --rm --interactive --tty --volume /example/path:/usr/src/code \
  --workdir /usr/src/code python:3.8.8 /bin/bash
```

```
root@751c47625400:/usr/src/code# ls
(files from /example/path on your host machine)
root@751c47625400:/usr/src/code#
```

The --volume /example/path:/usr/src/code option instructs docker to mount the files from /example/path on your host machine into the container at the destination location of /usr/src/code. The --workdir /usr/src/code argument tells docker to make /usr/src/code the working directory inside the container. The net result is that if you run ls inside of the container you should find all the files from /example/path in the Docker container. If you change /example/path to some path on your computer, you could run any Python code you have in that directory under Python 3.8.8 in the Docker container.

This book is not an introduction to Docker—it's an expansive technology—but using the preceding commands can be really useful when you want a temporary workspace to try something out in an isolated environment with any arbitrary version of Python that you want to use. I frequently use the commands you just learned about to try out different versions of Python, install pip packages in a temporary container workspace, and generally give myself a side-effect free sandbox. If you would like to learn more about Docker, the documentation on the official Python docker image page is an excellent interactive introduction.[16] Beyond that, you can peruse the official Docker documentation.[17]

You've now explored the interactive console and launched different versions of Python. In the next section we'll talk about one of the most important tools in your toolbox: pdb for debugging Python programs.

Investigating with pdb Breakpoints

Python includes a built-in debugger called pdb.[18] pdb allows you to halt your program's execution on any given line and use an interactive Python console to inspect your program's state. Since pdb is a built-in part of Python, you can import and use pdb at anytime without running additional external executables other than your program.

To add a breakpoint to your program, pick a target line and then add import pdb; pdb.set_trace() on that line. Up until now, we've been typing and/or pasting code into Python's interactive console, but for this example try running the following example code by saying python3 pdb_example.py:

```
pdb_example.py
def get_farm_animals():
    farm = ["cow", "pig", "goat"]
    return farm

import pdb; pdb.set_trace()  # add breakpoint
animals = ["otter", "seal"]
farm_animals = get_farm_animals()
animals = animals + farm_animals
print(animals)
```

pdb_example.py constructs a list of animals and prints it out. For our purposes, the most important part of pdb_example.py is that we set a breakpoint on line 5 using pdb. (The actual code in the file is just something for us to step through.)

---

16. https://hub.docker.com/_/python/
17. https://docs.docker.com
18. https://docs.python.org/3/library/pdb.html

After you execute python3 pdb_example.py, you should get dropped into an inter-active pdb session:

```
> /code/pdb_example.py(6)<module>()
-> animals = ["otter", "seal"]
(Pdb)
```

The program ran up until line number 6 (which binds animals to the list ["otter", "seal"]). The pdb.set_trace() call caused the program to halt and gave us the interactive pdb prompt shown earlier. Line 6 has not yet been executed, but would be next up as indicated by the arrow (->).

The breakpoint() Shortcut

 On Python 3.7 or newer, you can use the new built-in breakpoint() function to set a pdb trace. The default behavior of breakpoint() is to call import pdb; pdb.set_trace(), so using breakpoint() may save you a little typing.[19]

Let's get our bearings a little more by using the pdb command named list to print out the source code near our breakpoint:[20]

```
> /code/pdb_example.py(6)<module>()
-> animals = ["otter", "seal"]
(Pdb) list
  1     def get_farm_animals():
  2         farm = ["cow", "pig", "goat"]
  3         return farm
  4
  5     import pdb; pdb.set_trace()
  6  -> animals = ["otter", "seal"]
  7     farm_animals = get_farm_animals()
  8     animals = animals + farm_animals
  9     print(animals)
[EOF]
(Pdb)
```

Executing the list command prints out the nearby source code (in our case the entire file because pdb_example.py is so short). The arrow has not advanced, so we still have not executed any new code.

The pdb session—effectively—gives you a Python interactive console that allows you to inspect (and even manipulate) your program as it runs. Let's start by trying to inspect the animals variable:

---

19. https://docs.python.org/3/whatsnew/3.7.html#pep-553-built-in-breakpoint
20. https://docs.python.org/3/library/pdb.html

```
(Pdb) animals
*** NameError: name 'animals' is not defined
(Pdb)
```

Trying to get information about the animals variable resulted in the pdb session printing a NameError. As we learned earlier, our program stopped just before executing line 6, so the animals variable actually hasn't been assigned to any value yet. In order to advance our program so it executes line 6, we'll need to call the pdb command named next:

```
(Pdb) next
> /code/pdb_example.py(7)<module>()
-> farm_animals = get_farm_animals()
(Pdb) animals
['otter', 'seal']
(Pdb)
```

By running next, you advanced the program one line: line 6 was executed and the arrow now indicates that our current position is just before line 7. By typing animals and then Enter, you were able to output the repr of the animals variable (just as you learned about in code on page 4). pdb shows that animals was indeed bound to a list containing the strings otter and seal.

If we were to call next again, pdb would execute line 7 and farm_animals would be bound to the result of get_farm_animals(). But what if we wanted to investigate the interior of the get_farm_animals function itself? You can use the step command to instruct pdb to stop inside of a called function:

```
(Pdb) step
--Call--
> /code/pdb_example.py(1)get_farm_animals()
-> def get_farm_animals():
(Pdb) step
> /code/pdb_example.py(2)get_farm_animals()
-> farm = ["cow", "pig", "goat"]
(Pdb) list
  1     def get_farm_animals():
  2  ->     farm = ["cow", "pig", "goat"]
  3         return farm
  4
  5     import pdb; pdb.set_trace()
  6     animals = ["otter", "seal"]
  7     farm_animals = get_farm_animals()
  8     animals = animals + farm_animals
  9     print(animals)
[EOF]
(Pdb)
```

Calling step the first time shows the pdb is currently stopped at line 1 (where the function signature for get_farm_animals is defined). Calling step again moves pdb to just before line 2 that assigns the farm variable to a list of three elements. Calling list confirms our position by indicating that we are inside the get_farm_animals() function, about to execute line 2.

Quickly Run the Last pdb Command

If you are in a pdb session, just hitting Enter on a blank (Pdb) prompt line will automatically run the last pdb command again. So, for example, if the last command you ran was next, you can repeatedly hit Enter to continue running next until you arrive at a line where you would like to stop.

Congratulations, you have now learned the fundamentals of pdb. You are able to set a trace in code, output information about variables currently assigned into your program, advance your program's execution line by line using next, and jump into function calls using step.

Many developers use the print function liberally to debug their code and understand what is going on. pdb takes you one step beyond print debugging by dropping you into an interactive session where you can inspect your program's state without knowing beforehand exactly what variables and objects you want to print.

pdb has many useful commands beyond the few we've explored in this section so far. All of the commands are documented in Python's documentation,[21] but the following table summarizes the commands we've used so far and a select few of my favorites (marked with ✪):

Command	Shortcut	Result
list	l	Print source code near the current line
pp ✪	No short-cut	Pretty print the given expression, for example, 'pp some _variable'. Especially helpful when debugging long lists or nested dictionaries.
next	n	Execute until the next line is reached and then stop again
step	s	Same as next, but stops inside of called functions
where ✪	w	Print a stack trace indicating the current call stack

---

21. https://docs.python.org/3/library/pdb.html

Command	Shortcut	Result
return	r	Execute until the current function returns and then stop again
continue	c	Resume execution until the next breakpoint (if there are no more breakpoints, the program just continues normally)
quit	q	Quit debugger, program being executed is aborted

You'll notice that many of the commands include one or two letter shortcuts (for example, n for next) that allow you to run the command without typing out its full name. The shortcuts can help save you some typing when you are in a pdb session.

One of my favorites is the pp ("pretty print") shortcut. pp can help make longer data structures like a list of dictionaries more easily digestible by, for example, using discrete lines for each entry in a long list:

```
(Pdb) object_ids = [{"id": i} for i in range(8)]
(Pdb) object_ids
[{'id': 0}, {'id': 1}, {'id': 2}, {'id': 3}, {'id': 4}, {'id': 5},
{'id': 6}, {'id': 7}]
(Pdb) pp object_ids
[{'id': 0},
 {'id': 1},
 {'id': 2},
 {'id': 3},
 {'id': 4},
 {'id': 5},
 {'id': 6},
 {'id': 7}]
(Pdb)
```

The object_ids variable is bound to a list containing 8 dictionaries. Running pp object_ids outputs each entry on a separate line, making it easier to read.

Some pdb Commands Clash with Python Reserved Words

You may have noticed that some pdb commands clash with Python reserved names. For example, the pdb command list and the pdb command next both clash with Python reserved words: list is a built-in reserved for the list data structure, and next is a built-in function used in iteration.[a,b] (Similarly, the help pdb command clashes with the built-in function named help that you learned about earlier.)

These name clashes become problematic whenever you try to use, for example, list as an actual list instead of the pdb list command that prints source code. For example: if you try to convert range(3) into a list, you'll see a strange error:

```
(Pdb) list(range(3))
*** Error in argument: '(range(3))'
(Pdb)
```

pdb thinks you've tried to run its list command (and not Python's built-in data structure list). To work around this, you can use one of three alternatives.

1. Escape the pdb command with a ! character:

```
(Pdb) !list(range(3))
[0, 1, 2]
(Pdb)
```

2. Use the print function to avoid the collision in the first place:

```
(Pdb) print(list(range(3)))
[0, 1, 2]
(Pdb)
```

3. Use the pdb pretty print command pp:

```
(Pdb) pp list(range(3))
[0, 1, 2]
(Pdb)
```

---

a.   https://docs.python.org/3/tutorial/datastructures.html#more-on-lists
b.   https://docs.python.org/3/library/functions.html#next

You've run Python programs via the interactive console and debugged them using pdb. Next, we'll discuss strategies for reducing debugging by detecting bugs in your source code before you even try to run it.

Detecting Problems Early

Unlike traditionally compiled languages, Python does not require source code to be compiled into machine code before it is run. Instead, Python accepts source code directly and executes it as is. This means that it is possible for you to, for example, run invalid Python source code that never stands a chance of executing or working.

To reduce this risk, many Python projects run static analysis tools to help them validate and verify source code before trying to run it. What are static analysis tools? Static analysis tools don't actually run your code, but read it and inspect it for issues that can be found just by browsing the source code itself. Kind of like a friend peering over your shoulder as you type and letting you know when you've made a mistake before you've even tried to run anything.

In this section we'll talk about two tools for finding and eliminating bugs in your programs ahead of time: flake8 and mypy.

Running flake8 to Find Errors

The flake8 static analysis tool detects a number of different errors in Python source code and flags them for you to fix.[22] In this section, we'll highlight a select few errors flake8 detects to help you get a sense of flake8's benefits.

How Do I Run flake8?

 flake8 is a third-party package that you can install with Python's package manager pip.[23] If you're using this book's companion Docker image from Setting Up Your Environment and Using This Book's Companion Docker Image, on page 2, flake8 is already installed and ready to go—just type flake8 --help. If you're not using the companion image, we'll cover how to use pip in Running pip, on page 104. If you are already comfortable with pip and virtual environments, feel free to install flake8==3.8.4 and run it. Otherwise, it's okay to just follow along as we explore the capabilities of flake8.

Detecting Undefined Variables

flake8 detects, ahead of time, any Python source code that tries to access a variable that does not exist. For example, variable_does_not_exist.py contains a variable named oops that is never bound to a value:

variable_does_not_exist.py
```
Line 1  a = 1
     2
     3  # `a + oops` will never work:
     4  # Traceback (most recent call last):
     5  #   File "variable_does_not_exist.py", line 8, in <module>
     6  #     a + oops
     7  # NameError: name 'oops' is not defined
     8  a + oops
```

While variable_does_not_exist.py is valid syntactically, it will never run. a + oops will always raise an exception because the oops variable doesn't have a value.

flake8 is able to catch this error ahead of time. If you run flake8 against variable_does_not_exist.py by saying flake8 variable_does_not_exist.py, you'll see the following output:

❮ `variable_does_not_exist.py:8:5: F821 undefined name 'oops'`

---

22. https://flake8.pycqa.org/en/3.8.4/user/error-codes.html
23. https://pip.pypa.io/en/stable/

flake8 reports that it detects an error at line 8 column 5 of variable_does_not_exist.py. In particular, it detected that the oops variable is not defined (and so variable_does_not_exist.py will not be able to run successfully). Also included in the output is the code: F821. F821 is the code name flake8 uses to identify this error—allowing you to find all occurrences of a specific kind of error in your project.[24]

While the variable_does_not_exist.py file may seem a little trivial, problems like these tend to crop up relatively frequently especially as a Python codebase grows (or when developers decline to write tests for their code). Catching these errors ahead of time with flake8 spares you from bugs later.

Remove Wildcard Imports

flake8 detects when wildcard (*) imports are used and forbids them. For example, consider redefine_path.py which subtly and silently clobbers the value of the path variable:

```
redefine_path.py
Line 1 path = "/etc/hosts"
     2
     3 from os import *
     4
     5 print(path)
```

If you run python3 redefine_path.py you will receive output like the following:

```
<module 'posixpath' from '/usr/local/lib/python3.9/posixpath.py'>
```

Shouldn't the output have been /etc/hosts? Unfortunately, even though the path variable was initially bound to /etc/hosts, the path variable is clobbered to a new value when from os import * is run. This is because the os module itself includes a path module. So, when * is imported from os, the path module gets bound to the path variable and the /etc/hosts string effectively disappears without a trace. (Note that Python aliases os.path to an underlying module of posixpath if you are running on a POSIX system and ntpath if you are running on Windows).

flake8 forbids this variable clobbering situation from occurring at all. If you run flake8 redefine_path.py, one of the errors you'll see is:

```
redefine_path.py:3:1: F403 'from os import *' used; unable to detect
undefined names
```

flake8 detects an issue at line 3 column 1 saying that a wildcard (*) import is used, preventing flake8 from detecting undefined names. To resolve this error, you have to replace the * and import the exact names you are interested in

---

24. https://flake8.pycqa.org/en/3.8.4/user/error-codes.html

using. (For example, from os import environ if you wanted to use environ to get and set operating system environment variables.)

We'll discuss the dangers of wildcard imports in more detail in Dodging Wildcard Variable Shadowing, on page 119, but for now its enough to know that flake8 helps you detect and remove these before they manifest as dangerous bugs.

Prevent Duplicated Names

flake8 detects when you define a dictionary that repeats the same key multiple times with different values. Consider, for example, duplicate_dict_keys.py that defines two different values for the "pi" key in my_dict:

```
duplicate_dict_keys.py
Line 1  my_dict = {"pi": 3.14, "pi": "apple"}
     2
     3  # is this `3.14 * 5` or `"apple" * 5` ??
     4  print(my_dict["pi"] * 5)
```

The existing code is—at best—ambiguous. Should my_dict["pi"] return 3.14, or should it return "apple"? At the end of the day, a dictionary data structure only allows the "pi" key to appear once, so only one of 3.14 and "apple" will actually stick and win out as the value.

If you run flake8 duplicate_dict_keys.py, flake8 will catch and suggest you fix the key duplication ahead of time:

```
duplicate_dict_keys.py:1:12: F601 dictionary key 'pi' repeated with
different values
duplicate_dict_keys.py:1:24: F601 dictionary key 'pi' repeated with
different values
```

flake8 indicates the two locations on line 1 that assign the 'pi' key to a different value and suggests you address the duplication. Again, while the duplicate_dict_keys.py example may feel a little contrived because it is so small, this check becomes especially helpful when your codebase defines many dictionary literals—especially ones with dozens, hundreds, or even thousands of keys.

Prevent Duplicated Names Part 2: Tests

flake8 uses a similar duplicate detection scheme that can help you catch issues with tests as well.

After introducing flake8 to a codebase at a new job, I was simultaneously relieved and horrified when flake8 detected some tests that were being implicitly skipped. Consider the following simplified example of a unittest TestCase that tests math operations:

duplicate_tests.py
```
Line 1  import unittest
2
3
4  class TestMath(unittest.TestCase):
5      def test_add_1(self):
6          self.assertEqual(1 + 1, 2)
7
8      def test_add_1(self):
9          self.assertEqual(1 - 1, 0)
```

duplicate_tests.py defines a TestCase class named TestMath that—supposedly—tests that both 1 + 1 = 2 and 1 - 1 = 0. Unfortunately, if you actually run this test file with the unittest standard library module, you'll see that only one test runs:

```
python3 -m unittest duplicate_tests.py
```

```
.
----------------------------------------------------------------------
Ran 1 test in 0.000s

OK
```

The test output indicates that it only Ran 1 test despite our code defining two tests. Similar to the duplicate dictionary key example shown earlier, only one method of a given name can ultimately bind to a class object. In this case there are two methods named test_add_1 that each try to bind to the TestMath class. However, since only one of the test_add_1 methods can get bound to the class, only one test actually runs.

When a large project accumulates many tests, and developers have accidentally written tests that have the same name, it's easy to miss this kind of problem. It's dangerous when code that developers thought was covered with tests actually isn't.

flake8 helps you avoid skipping tests by flagging the duplicated names. If you run flake8 duplicate_tests.py, you'll see an error message like this:

```
duplicate_tests.py:8:5: F811 redefinition of unused 'test_add_1' from line 5
```

flake8 notes that test_add_1 has been redefined on line 8. If you fix this issue by, for example, changing the name of the test on line 8 to test_subtract_1, flake8 will stop complaining and two tests will run:

duplicate_tests_fixed.py
```
Line 1  import unittest
2
3
4  class TestMath(unittest.TestCase):
5      def test_add_1(self):
6          self.assertEqual(1 + 1, 2)
```

```
7
8    def test_subtract_1(self):
9        self.assertEqual(1 - 1, 0)
```

After renaming the second test_add_1 to test_subtract_1, using the unittest module to execute the tests results in both tests actually executing:

```
python3 -m unittest duplicate_tests_fixed.py
```

```
..
------------------------------------------------------------------
Ran 2 tests in 0.000s

OK
```

Running Additional Checks with flake8-bugbear

There a number of available add-ons that you can use to augment flake8. I highly recommend one add-on in particular: flake-bugbear. flake8-bugbear[25] allows flake8 to detect a few more classes of errors and mistakes. In particular, flake8-bugbear automatically flags instances of the mutable default argument trap and helps you eliminate them from your codebase. The mutable default argument trap is covered in Binding Early: Problems with Default Arguments, on page 99. Don't worry too much about the mutable default argument trap now—just know that flake8-bugbear will help you automatically eliminate it.

Any Python project should use flake8 and flake8-bugbear to prevent errors in its code. I highly recommend adding flake8 and flake8-bugbear to your development flow (for example, in your continuous integration server) to prevent committing code with bugs that flake8 can spare you from. (Be sure to run flake8 with its --select=F option if you want to ignore flake8's style suggestions and only enable its error detection.[26])

In the next section we'll introduce another tool that belongs in your Python development flow: mypy.

Running mypy for Optimistic Type Checking

Python does not enforce strict typing controls. If, for example, a function accepts an integer as an input, Python will not complain if you pass that function string as input instead. Python will try to run anything, even if it might crash or produce an unexpected result.

In the past few years, however, Python has added support for including type annotations in source code. Type annotations, which we'll see examples of

---

25. https://pypi.org/project/flake8-bugbear/
26. https://flake8.pycqa.org/en/3.8.4/user/violations.html#selecting-violations-with-flake8

next, are not inspected by Python at runtime at all. Type annotations, however, serve as fodder for the gradual type checker called mypy.[27]

The mypy tool reads your source code and makes guesses about types in your program based on your type annotations, type annotations in the standard library, type annotations in third-party packages, and its general understanding of Python syntax. Based on this collection of inferences, mypy performs some optimistic checks ahead of time to verify that your program passes around expected data types and uses them in ways that are valid. I say optimistic because, again, none of these typing checks are enforced at runtime. So, its always possible mypy won't be able to understand the entirety of your program, or foresee an impish part of your program that spews bad types into the call stack.

mypy is gradual in the sense that your entire program doesn't have to be type annotated. If you only type annotate a few objects, mypy will do its best with those annotations and its other derived knowledge. The more type annotations you add, the better chance mypy has for success, but you can add as much or as little as you like.

Detecting Mismatched Types

In one of its most fundamental behaviors, mypy detects when the wrong type of variable is passed to a type annotated function:

```
wrong_argument_type.py
object_info = {
    "123": {"description": "example object"},
    "456": {"description": "another example object"},
}

def print_object_info(object_id: str):
    info = object_info.get(object_id, default=f"{object_id} not found")
    print(info)

print_object_info(object_id=123)
```

wrong_argument_type.py defines a function print_object_info that expects its object_id argument to be a str as denoted by the type annotation syntax of : <type>. The call to print_object_info at the end of the file, however, tries to pass an int argument for object_id. If you run mypy against this file by saying mypy wrong_argument_type.py, it will complain about the type mismatch:

```
wrong_argument_type.py:10: error: Argument "object_id" to
"print_object_info" has incompatible type "int"; expected "str"
```

---

27. https://github.com/python/mypy

Indeed, mypy indicates that on line 10 the object_id argument is unexpectedly supplied as an int instead of a str.

How Do I Run mypy?

 mypy is a package that you can install with Python's package manager pip.[28] If you're using this book's companion Docker image from Setting Up Your Environment and Using This Book's Companion Docker Image, on page 2, mypy is already installed and ready to go—just type mypy --help. If you're not using the companion image, we'll cover how to use pip in Running pip, on page 104. If you are already comfortable with pip and virtual environments, feel free to install mypy==0.790 and run it. Otherwise, it's ok to just follow along as we explore the capabilities of mypy.

Finding Unsupported Arguments

mypy builds on its argument type checking ability and also notes if you supply an unsupported argument to a function:

```
unsupported_argument.py
object_info = {
    "123": {"description": "example object"},
    "456": {"description": "another example object"},
}

def print_object_info(object_id: str):
    info = object_info.get(object_id, default=f"{object_id} not found")
    print(info)

print_object_info(this_is_not_an_argument="oops")
```

If you run mypy unsupported_argument.py, you'll see an error like this:

```
unsupported_argument.py:10: error: Unexpected keyword argument
"this_is_not_an_argument" for "print_object_info"
```

mypy indicates with an error that this_is_not_an_argument is unexpected (because print_object_info doesn't support such an argument). While neither of the two checks we've introduced so far may seem revolutionary or all powerful, they start to add up as your Python project grows. It can be especially helpful to have mypy's extra set of eyes when you need to make large scale changes that modify many lines at once. The more code you have, the more likely it is you'll make a mistake. mypy is always there to catch you.

---

28. https://pip.pypa.io/en/stable/

Checking Code That Doesn't Have Type Annotations

Since mypy knows about Python's standard library, it can detect issues even if the code under check doesn't include type annotations. For example, running mypy bad_string_method.py detects an issue with this attempted str method call:

```
bad_string_method.py
some_string = "ABC"
some_string.foo_bar()
```

```
bad_string_method.py:2: error: "str" has no attribute "foo_bar"
```

In the preceding example, the variable some_string is bound to the value "ABC". Trying to call the nonexistent method foo_bar will eventually raise an exception if you try to run the code. mypy, however, can catch this ahead of time and indicate that foo_bar is not an available attribute. Note that we didn't add any explicit type annotations in this code: mypy uses its knowledge of the Python language and the standard library to add coverage for us. mypy automatically detected that some_string was bound to a str type and used that knowledge to flag an error that foo_bar was not available for use.

Encouraging Consistent and Explicit Type Usage

mypy can also make slightly more subtle recommendations based on its reading of your source code. For example, mypy frowns on swapping the type associated with a variable:

```
change_type.py
Line 1  def print_details(level: int):
            user_object = {
                "id": "2",
                "name": "David",
    5           "favorite_color": "blue",
            }
            if level <= 1:
                keys = ["id", "name"]
            else:
    10          keys = ("id", "name", "favorite_color")

            print(" ".join(user_object[k] for k in keys))
```

In the preceding example, the keys variable controls what dictionary elements are printed out—more details are printed out if level is greater than 1. keys is conditionally assigned to either a list (on line 8) of strings or a tuple of strings (on line 10). If you run mypy change_type.py, mypy complains about this dynamism:

```
change_type.py:10: error: Incompatible types in assignment (expression has
type "Tuple[str, str, str]", variable has type "List[str]")
```

mypy notes that keys is initially bound to a List[str] (list of strings) type, but then is potentially later adjusted to being Tuple[str, str, str] (a tuple of three strings). One way to fix this complaint is to explicitly inform mypy that either List[str] or Tuple[str, str, str] are expected:

```
change_type_fixed.py
from typing import List, Tuple, Union

def print_details(level: int):
    user_object = {
        "id": "2",
        "name": "David",
        "favorite_color": "blue",
    }
    keys: Union[List[str], Tuple[str, str, str]]
    if level <= 1:
        keys = ["id", "name"]
    else:
        keys = ("id", "name", "favorite_color")

    print(" ".join(user_object[k] for k in keys))
```

keys: Union[List[str], Tuple[str, str, str]] on line 9 is a type annotation that allows us to mark keys as either being a list of strings or a tuple of three strings. Providing this hint satisfies mypy that our code is clearly type annotated and behaving as expected—if you run mypy change_type_fixed.py, mypy will report no errors.

As you might expect, you could also only ever bind one type to the keys variable to fix this error. For example, if you always bind keys to a list, mypy will no longer complain about changing types:

```
change_type_fixed_2.py
def print_details(level: int):
    user_object = {
        "id": "2",
        "name": "David",
        "favorite_color": "blue",
    }
    if level <= 1:
        keys = ["id", "name"]
    else:
        keys = ["id", "name", "favorite_color"]

    print(" ".join(user_object[k] for k in keys))
```

This solution satisfies mypy and is much less verbose than adding the long type hint of keys: Union[List[str], Tuple[str, str, str]].

The first time I saw recommendations like these from mypy, I was a little taken aback. So what if I used a list for one assignment and a tuple for the other—the code worked out the same. One of Python's strengths, after all, is not having to rigorously define types. It was only when I applied mypy against a larger codebase that I started to feel the benefits. I saw places where the type assigned to a variable would swing wildly line by line and sometimes be inappropriately handled in later sections of code. mypy forced our team to confront these code sections, explicitly indicate types (fixing downstream bugs along the way). Our code became clearer to read and also less bug prone.

mypy is certainly not required for a successful Python project—dynamism is inherent to Python and tends to be one of its strongest features. In my experience though, mypy (when enforced in a CI system, for example) over time helps cut down bugs and subtly nudges developers toward patterns that more clearly indicate the types involved. Additionally, using type annotations has the added benefit of leaving small documentation clues to teammates in the future. This can be especially helpful in situations where the types expected as inputs for some function aren't abundantly obvious.

You can visit the mypy cheatsheet for a great list of quick examples to get you started adding type annotations throughout your code.[29]

You've now learned about flake8, flake-bugbear, and mypy. All three of these tools—I believe—are essential tools for your Python project. If you avoid committing code that these tools flag as suspicious, your code will improve, and your bug count will decrease.

In the next section we'll discuss using a tool to automatically format your code so it looks uniform.

Formatting and Styling Your Code Consistently

Using a program to automatically format code won't necessarily prevent bugs, but it can improve the maintainability of your project over time by bringing consistency, readability, and reducing the number of "tabs versus spaces" style arguments your team has. Some languages include automatic code formatters as part of their implementation—go comes with gofmt, for example.

Python does not have a built-in mechanism for formatting code like go does, but a tool named black[30] is the Python Software Foundation's "blessed" application for automatically formatting Python code.[31] black should be one of the tools in your tool box, and many popular Python projects and corporations

29. https://mypy.readthedocs.io/en/stable/cheat_sheet_py3.html
30. https://black.readthedocs.io/en/stable/
31. https://twitter.com/llanga/status/1123980466292445190

(for example, Dropbox, Facebook, and Mozilla) use black to automatically format their Python code.

black bills itself as, "the uncompromising Python code formatter." In general, it cannot be configured or have any of its formatting behaviors meaningfully changed. It formats Python code the way it will, and you are required to accept it. Its name was inspired by a Henry Ford quote about paint on the Model T: "Any customer can have a car painted any color that he wants so long as it is black."[32] Jokes aside, black generally formats code in ways that are pleasant, readable, and consistent.

Many code formatters promise to stop arguments between teammates over code style, and black has lived up to that promise, but black is particularly effective at stopping yourself from arguing with yourself—you can type code quickly (and "lazily") because black will automatically format anything you write.

Like flake8 and mypy, you should include black in your development workflow (or continuous integration server) to ensure that all your code is formatted consistently.

Formatting Code with black

In the next section we'll go over a few examples of code formatted by black to get an idea of its general style.

How Do I Run black?

black is a package that you can install with Python's package manager pip.[33] If you're using this book's companion Docker image from Setting Up Your Environment and Using This Book's Companion Docker Image, on page 2, black is already installed and ready to go—just type black --help. If you're not using the companion image, we'll cover how to use pip in Running pip, on page 104. If you are already comfortable with pip and virtual environments, feel free to install black==20.8b1 and run it. Otherwise, it's ok to just follow along as we explore the capabilities of black.

---

black intelligently breaks long Boolean conditionals into multiple lines with leading binary operators (as per the latest guidance from Python's style guide):[34]

---

32. https://en.wikiquote.org/wiki/Henry_Ford

33. https://pip.pypa.io/en/stable/

34. https://www.python.org/dev/peps/pep-0008/#should-a-line-break-before-or-after-a-binary-operator

```
# before black:
def my_function(**options):
    if options.get("option_a") and options.get("option_b") and not \
    options.get("option_c"):
        return True
    return False
```

```
# after black:
def my_function(**options):
    if (
        options.get("option_a")
        and options.get("option_b")
        and not options.get("option_c")
    ):
        return True
    return False
```

Helpfully, the black formatted code doesn't slam three conditionals into one exceptionally long line. Instead, it separates each condition onto a more manageable line and puts the binary operator (in this case and) at the beginning of each line.

Similarly, black will split long literals onto multiple lines:

```
# before black:
def my_function():
    my_dict = {"my key": 'my value', "another key": 'another value', \
    "third key": "value 3"}
    return my_dict
```

```
# after black:
def my_function():
    my_dict = {
        "my key": "my value",
        "another key": "another value",
        "third key": "value 3",
    }
    return my_dict
```

black spreads the my_dict dictionary literal over multiple lines instead of the previous run-on line.

Notably, black will also perform the opposite procedure; black will condense literals if they don't exceed black's line length limit:

```
# before black:
def my_function():
    my_list = [
        1,
        2
    ]
    return my_list
```

```
# after black:
def my_function():
    my_list = [1, 2]
    return my_list
```

Since the my_list literal fits on one line according to black's line length limit, the black formatted code condenses the code slightly.

black will also format function call chains across multiple lines in a highly readable way:

```
# before black:
def get_user_from_database(user_id):
    return db.query(models.User.id).filter(models.User.id == user_id).\
        order_by(models.User.id.asc()).\
        first()
```

```
# after black:
def get_user_from_database(user_id):
    return (
        database.query(models.User.id)
        .filter(models.User == user_id)
        .order_by(models.User.id.asc())
        .first()
    )
```

This sort of formatting can be especially helpful in applications that do a lot of database work with an ORM (like those provided by Django and SQLAlchemy), or any other tool that involves long chains of function calls.[35]

Now that you've seen some of the benenfits of black, consider running black . -- check in your build system to ensure that only code formatted by black can be successfully committed into your repository. And, of course, consider adding black to your local text editing workflow so you can constantly and painlessly reformat your code as you write it.

---

black Code Formatting in This Book

The Python code in this book is—for the most part—automatically formatted with black. Due to printing constraints on white space and line length, however, some code in this book isn't strictly black compliant (small creative liberties were taken to meet requirements for this book's production printing).

---

35. https://en.wikipedia.org/wiki/Object-relational_mapping

Wrapping Up

You've explored a lot of Python in this first chapter. You used docker as a convenient way to experiment with different python environments, pdb to interactively debug code execution without print, and the combination of flake8 + mypy + black to automatically format your code and proactively squash bugs.

Now that we have the ability to run Python and audit our Python with static analysis tools, we can look into key selections from Python's standard library in the next chapter.

## CHAPTER 2

Shifting Up with the Standard Library

I've had one bad bicycling accident in my life. I wasn't technically on a bike when I got hurt. My four-year-old self was running toward my bike to go for a ride when I tripped and fell directly against the handlebars. My parents took me to the emergency room, where I had to get stitches on my lip. In retrospect, I'm not sure who was more terrified—me or my parents.

In my life since then, I've been fortunate enough to ride all manner of bikes without major injury: bikes with disc brakes, bikes fully suspended over front and rear shock absorbers, oversized mountain bikes with 29" diameter tires, and even bikes with electrically assisted pedals. Outside of the early accident, many of my best memories are from spending time on bikes. Summers spent with friends riding in the sun, biking around campus in college, mountain biking in the foothills near my home.

I like to think of Python's standard library as a sort of bike. It's a tremendous machine that provides a gateway to a wealth of experience and abilities—along with some requisite danger. The first time you ride a bike or write Python, you might fall or otherwise hurt yourself. But, as you learn to ride you find yourself with the freedom to go anywhere you want and the confidence to go to those places: you have mastered a powerful tool.

In the last chapter, you learned how to interact with Python generally and how to catch bugs before you even ran code. In this chapter, we'll get more specific and focus on some of the finer modules in the standard library. Though this chapter can't and won't cover all of the standard library, it will go over a selection of tremendously useful tools that you can use in your projects to great benefit. In particular, we'll discuss the collections module, tempfile, subprocess, sqlite3, and even profiling code with cProfile.

Using the collections Module for Concise Code

The collections standard library module is a standby for many Python developers. It provides a number of utilities (particularly defaultdict, Counter, and namedtuple) that help reduce boilerplate code and make it possible to write concise Python. After you read through this section on collections, you will be familiar with some of the utilities in the module and be prepared to include them in your projects.

Write Concise Code with defaultdict

defaultdict is a convenience provided by the collections module. defaultdict allows you to add values to dictionaries concisely and reduce boilerplate code.

Consider, for example, if you had a program that used a dict to map file owners to files. The following script takes a list of (owner, file_name) pairs and collects them in a dictionary with owners as keys and lists of file names as values:

file_owners.py
```
files = [
    ("Jack", "hill.txt"),
    ("Jill", "water.txt"),
    ("Jack", "crown.txt"),
]

owner_to_files = {}
for owner, file_name in files:
    if owner not in owner_to_files:
        owner_to_files[owner] = []
    owner_to_files[owner].append(file_name)

print(owner_to_files)
```

file_owners.py defines a list named files that consists of three pairs of strings, each with a file name and the owner of that file. Jack owns two files (hill.txt + crown.txt) and Jill owns one file (water.txt). The for loop iterates over the owner, file_name pairs in files and updates the owner_to_files dictionary accordingly—each unique file owner is a key in the dictionary mapped to a list of the file names they own. The body of the for loop is careful to only run owner_to_files[owner].append(file_name) after it has added an empty to list as the value for any owner not already in owner_to_files.

If you run python3 file_owners.py, you should see the following output:

```
{'Jack': ['hill.txt', 'crown.txt'], 'Jill': ['water.txt']}
```

defaultdict can help slim down this example and make it slightly more concise especially in the body of the for loop. file_owners_default_dict.py modifies file_owners.py slightly so that it uses a defaultdict to group lists of files with their owner in a dict:

```python
file_owners_default_dict.py
from collections import defaultdict

files = [
    ("Jack", "hill.txt"),
    ("Jill", "water.txt"),
    ("Jack", "crown.txt"),
]

owner_to_files = defaultdict(list)
for owner, file_name in files:
    owner_to_files[owner].append(file_name)

print(owner_to_files)
```

If you run python3 file_owners_default_dict.py, you still receive effectively the same result (Jack owning hill.txt + crown.txt and Jill owning water.txt):

```
defaultdict(<class 'list'>, {'Jack': ['hill.txt', 'crown.txt'], 'Jill':
['water.txt']})
```

A few things have changed, though. First of all, you imported defaultdict from the collections standard library module. You then bound owner_to_files to the result of defaultdict(list). The for loop also now only has one line in its body: a line that unconditionally calls owner_to_files[owner].append(file_name). The output still maps 'Jack' and 'Jill' to the appropriate lists of files, but there is a bit more debug information. In particular, the output starts with defaultdict(<class 'list'>) where before it just started immediately with the representation of the dict.

Generally, the outcome is that your code is more concise and has fewer lines (one in the for loop body instead of three). But how is this possible and what does defaultdict(list) and its debug string companion defaultdict(<class 'list'>) mean? Let's explore this now.

defaultdict is, itself, a function. The first argument to the defaultdict function is another function: in particular, a factory function that will produce default values in the resulting dict. For our factory function, we pass the Python built-in function list (which—when called—returns a new empty list object).[1] In other words, defaultdict(list) (displayed as defaultdict(<class 'list'>) in debugging output) runs list() anytime a regular dict would ordinarily raise a KeyError:

```python
>>> from collections import defaultdict
>>> regular_dict = {}
>>> regular_dict['key']
```

---

1. https://docs.python.org/3/library/functions.html#func-list

```
Traceback (most recent call last):
  File "<stdin>", line 1, in <module>
KeyError: 'key'
>>> example_default_dict = defaultdict(list)
>>> example_default_dict['key']
[]
>>>
```

In the preceding example, you bind the variable regular_dict to a standard and empty Python dictionary. Since regular_dict contains no entries, trying to retrieve the value stored at 'key' results in a KeyError Exception. The defaultdict bound to example_default_dict behaves differently than regular_dict. Even though example_default_dict also starts off empty, accessing 'key' returns an empty list.

As you saw in file_owners_default_dict.py, you can take advantage of this behavior to immediately call the append method on a list even if you aren't sure that the given key is present already:

```
>>> from collections import defaultdict
>>> owner_to_files = defaultdict(list)
>>> owner_to_files["Jack"].append("tumble.txt")
>>> owner_to_files
defaultdict(<class 'list'>, {'Jack': ['tumble.txt']})
>>>
```

The preceding example demonstrates the same behavior you already saw in file_owners_default_dict.py: defaultdict(list) automatically inserts an empty list when a regular dict would otherwise raise a KeyError exception. You can actually use defaultdict with factory functions other than list, as you'll see next.

Using defaultdict with Other Data Types

In the previous section, you used defaultdict(list) to create a dictionary that would automatically call list() (thereby inserting a new empty list) anytime you tried to access a key that wasn't present in the underlying dictionary. You can pass arguments other than list to the defaultdict function to automatically add different default values.

For example, instead of list you could use set to automatically insert empty set objects anytime there would otherwise have been a KeyError:

```
>>> from collections import defaultdict
>>> example_set_default_dict = defaultdict(set)
>>> example_set_default_dict['friends'].add('Jack')
>>> example_set_default_dict['friends'].add('Jill')
>>> example_set_default_dict['friends'].add('Jack')
>>> example_set_default_dict['friends']
{'Jack', 'Jill'}
>>>
```

Binding the variable named example_set_default_dict to defaultdict(set) creates a defaultdict that will automatically call set() to insert an empty set anytime there would have otherwise been a KeyError. In the preceding example, 'Jack', 'Jill', and 'Jack' (again) are added to a set that is automatically created the first time the 'friends' key is accessed.[2] Since set data structures cannot have repeated elements, the final value of the set is just {'Jack', 'Jill'}.

Even the datatype int can be used in defaultdict to create a dictionary that automatically adds 0 anytime there would otherwise be a KeyError:

```
>>> from collections import defaultdict
>>> int()
0
>>> example_int_default_dict = defaultdict(int)
>>> example_int_default_dict["total"] += 1
>>> example_int_default_dict["total"] += 1
>>> example_int_default_dict["total"]
2
>>>
```

The beginning of this sample code demonstrates that calling the built-in datatype int by saying int() returns 0. When you bind defaultdict(int) to the variable example_int_default_dict, you are essentially instructing defaultdict to insert int() (a.k.a. 0) anytime there would otherwise be a KeyError. So, when you access the "total" key, you can immediately start adding to it. By adding to "total" twice you wind up executing 0 + 1 + 1 and producing 2 as your final output.

While this counting problem is solvable with defaultdicts, because it comes up so often there's actually a way to express this even more concisely: collections.Counter.

Use Counter for Tallying

The collections module also provides a class called Counter that you can use to maintain tallies. You can, for example, get tallies for all the unique entries in a list:

```
>>> from collections import Counter
>>> counter = Counter(["dog", "cat", "dog"])
>>> counter
Counter({'dog': 2, 'cat': 1})
>>> counter['dog']
2
>>>
```

---

2.   https://docs.python.org/3/library/stdtypes.html#frozenset.add

The counter object behaves like a dict, allowing you to retrieve tallies for different entries like the two occurrences of 'dog'. In addition, you can also call the update method on a Counter to add more tallies to an existing Counter and use the most_common method to get a list of tuples with the entries ordered by frequency:

```
>>> from collections import Counter
>>> counter = Counter(["fox", "wolf", "wolf"])
>>> counter.update(["bear", "bear", "wolf"])
>>> counter.most_common()
[('wolf', 3), ('bear', 2), ('fox', 1)]
>>>
```

You've seen just how convenient defaultdict and Counter from the collections module can be to use. We'll explore another collections tool next: namedtuple.

Create Resilient Classes with namedtuple

The namedtuple function from the collections module provides a way to wrangle Python's tuple data structure into useful little classes.[3] Before we get into namedtuple, let's take a brief detour to learn about some of the benefits of tuples in general.

Exploring the Benefits of Python's tuple Data Structure

In Python, you can use the tuple type to create sequences of fixed size—sequences where elements cannot be added or removed. Although elements held in tuples may themselves be mutable (in other words, putting a list inside a tuple does not suddenly make the list immutable), tuples themselves are immutable. tuples can be helpful for strongly associating multiple objects together with the confidence that they'll stay associated—for example, representing database rows or configuration values.

Let's consider some example tuples that represent three pieces of information about a running program (commit, branch, Python version):

```
>>> program_info_a = ("b3607e5", "main", "3.9.2")
>>> program_info_a[0]
'b3607e5'
>>> program_info_a[1]
'main'
>>> program_info_a[0]
'3.9.2'
>>> program_info_a[0] = "new value"
Traceback (most recent call last):
  File "<stdin>", line 1, in <module>
```

---

3.   https://docs.python.org/3/tutorial/datastructures.html#tuples-and-sequences

```
TypeError: 'tuple' object does not support item assignment
>>> program_info_b = ("b3607e5", "main", "3.9.2")
>>> program_info_a == program_info_b
True
>>> dict_example = {program_info_a: 'a'}
>>> dict_example[program_info_a]
'a'
>>> dict_example[program_info_b]
'a'
>>>
```

As you just learned, tuple does not support element reassignment. So when you run program_info_a[0] = "new value", Python raises a TypeError to forbid the reassignment. In addition, tuples with identical elements are considered equivalent and will hash to the same value. That's why program_info_a == program_info_b returns True and why looking up both program_info_a and program_info_b in dict_example always yields the 'a' value.

The ("b3607e5", "main", "3.9.2") representing (commit, branch, Python version) might be a useful object to have in our application to encapsulate how a program is running. However, remembering that the commit is always stored at index 0, the branch is stored at index 1, and the Python version at index 2 will make our data structure opaque and less friendly to application code and developers. Enter: the namedtuple function provided by the collections module.

Making Friendlier tuples Using namedtuple

namedtuple takes a series of arguments and returns a new tuple subclass that your program can use. Let's try out namedtuple quickly in the interactive console to create a class that holds our three program configuration values:

```
>>> from collections import namedtuple
>>> field_names = ["commit", "branch", "python_version"]
>>> ProgramInfo = namedtuple("ProgramInfo", field_names=field_names)
>>> ProgramInfo()
Traceback (most recent call last):
  File "<stdin>", line 1, in <module>
TypeError: __new__() missing 3 required positional arguments: 'commit',
'branch', and 'python_version'
```

In this example, we call the namedtuple function with two arguments: the string "ProgramInfo" and a list of three strings for field_names. namedtuple uses the first argument (the "ProgramInfo" string) to determine the name of the new class it returns. namedtuple uses the list of field_names to determine what fields the returned class should support. When we try to instantiate a ProgramInfo instance by saying ProgramInfo(), we get an error saying that we need to provide three arguments to instantiate the object. Let's see how we can rectify this error and successfully create a new ProgramInfo object:

```
>>> info = ProgramInfo(commit="abc", branch="main", python_version="3.9.2")
>>> info
ProgramInfo(commit='abc', branch='main', python_version='3.9.2')
>>> info.branch
'main'
>>>
```

After providing values for commit, branch, and python_version we are able to successfully instantiate a ProgramInfo object named info. Accessing info.branch retrieves the value of 'main' that we set when the object was constructed. Let's extend on the work you've just done in the interactive console and work with Program-Info a little more closely:

```
program_info.py
import os
import platform
from collections import import namedtuple

ProgramInfo = namedtuple(
    "ProgramInfo",
    field_names=["commit", "branch", "python_version"]
)


def get_program_info():
    return ProgramInfo(
        commit=os.environ.get("COMMIT", "unknown"),
        branch=os.environ.get("BRANCH", "unknown"),
        python_version=platform.python_version(),
    )
```

If you paste the preceding code into a Python interactive console and then run

```
print(get_program_info())
```

you should receive output like the following:

```
ProgramInfo(commit='unknown', branch='unknown', python_version='3.9.2')
```

The function get_program_info returns a new instance of the ProgramInfo class filled in with some values. Note that the value associated to python_version will vary depending on what version of Python you are running. (commit and branch are set to "unknown" in this example, but might represent a Git commit and Git branch in a project using Git version control.)

OK, so we created a tuple subclass with three fields. Did we really gain anything, though? Yes, our new ProgramInfo has a number of benefits, including the following:

1. ProgramInfo creates an _init_ that requires values for all given field_names.
2. ProgramInfo automatically generates a friendly debug string.
3. ProgramInfo instances prevent field reassignment.
4. ProgramInfo includes equality and hash support for free.

You've actually just seen the benefits of items 1 and 2 on the list. To instantiate a ProgramInfo instance you had to provide values for commit, branch, and python_version (which were the given field names for ProgramInfo). Additionally, when you ran print(get_program_info()), you saw a nice string representation of the ProgramInfo object that detailed the values for commit, branch, and python_version. When you learned about the tuple data structure at the beginning of this section, you also got a preview of benefits 3 and 4.

Helpfully, the ProgramInfo debug string is more useful than the debug string of standard Python classes:

```
>>> class ExampleClass:
...     example = "value"
...
>>> print(ExampleClass())
<__main__.ExampleClass object at 0x7f3ab925bbe0>
>>>
```

When you define a standard python class like ExampleClass in the preceding code, the standard debug string isn't particularly helpful: you see the name of the class and where it is stored in memory (the 0x7f3ab... part of the string). Neither of these are as useful as a debug string like ProgramInfo(commit='unknown', branch='unknown', python_version='3.9.2'), which gives you a full sense of the object.

Now that we've gone over the first two advantages (autogenerated _init_ and helpful debug strings), let's talk about the namedtuple benefits 3 and 4—field reassignment prevention, and equality and hash support—in a little more detail.

Preventing Field Reassignments with namedtuple

Since the namedtuple function returns a subclass of the tuple data type, ProgramInfo's fields cannot be assigned new values:

```
prog_info = get_program_info()
prog_info.commit = "this line will raise an Exception"
```

As earlier, if you paste program_info.py into your interactive console, and then run the preceding code, you should receive the following output:

```
Traceback (most recent call last):
  File "<stdin>", line 1, in <module>
AttributeError: can't set attribute
```

Trying to change the commit field on the ProgramInfo instance prog_info causes an AttributeError to be raised. This is helpful for prog_info because it prevents other parts of the program from changing the values of commit, or branch, or python_version. Since commit, branch, and python_version can't really change in the course of a Python process, the assignment prevention in prog_info nicely matches the real-world constraints.

An alternative implementation of ProgramInfo using a regular class would not benefit from the same field reassignment protection:

program_info_class.py
```python
import os
import platform

class ProgramInfoClass:
    def __init__(self, commit, branch, python_version):
        self.commit = commit
        self.branch = branch
        self.python_version = python_version

def get_program_info_class():
    return ProgramInfoClass(
        commit=os.environ.get("COMMIT", "unknown"),
        branch=os.environ.get("BRANCH", "unknown"),
        python_version=platform.python_version(),
    )
```

If you paste this into a Python interactive console and then run the following:

```python
prog_info_class_based = get_program_info_class()
print(prog_info_class_based.commit)
prog_info_class_based.commit = "oops"
print(prog_info_class_based.commit)
```

you should receive output like this:

```
unknown
oops
```

program_info_class.py defines a class named ProgramInfoClass. ProgramInfoClass is analogous to ProgramInfo in that it also tracks commit, branch, and python_version fields. Since ProgramInfoClass, however, is a standard Python class, it does not protect its attributes from mutation (something we will discuss more in Maintaining Privacy in a Public World, on page 112). This means that no exception is raised when the commit field is changed from its initial value of unknown to the new value of oops.

Preventing these reassignments makes namedtuple classes (like ProgramInfo) especially useful for configuration objects that should not be changed (for example, database connection parameters or a configuration object for an application).

Now that you've seen namedtuple's useful debug string and attribute reassignment prevention, you are ready to explore a third benefit of namedtuple in the next section.

Getting Equality and Hash Support for Free with namedtuple

The ProgramInfo namedtuple that we first defined in code on page 40 includes built-in support for equality and hashing. Consider, for example, if we created two ProgramInfo instances with the same attributes and compared them:

```
>>> program_info_a = get_program_info()
>>> program_info_b = get_program_info()
>>> print(program_info_a)
ProgramInfo(commit='unknown', branch='unknown', python_version='3.9.2')
>>> print(program_info_b)
ProgramInfo(commit='unknown', branch='unknown', python_version='3.9.2')
>>> program_info_a == program_info_b
True
>>>
```

In this example, program_info_a and program_info_b are both ProgramInfo namedtuple instances with identical values for their attributes. If we compare program_info_a with program_info_b using Python's == equality operator, Python indicates that the two instances are equivalent by returning True.

It's worth noting that two namedtuple instances bound to different class names with identical attributes will also compare equal. Consider the following example where OtherNamedTuple is created to also hold three elements:

```
>>> program_info_a = get_program_info()
>>> print(program_info_a)
ProgramInfo(commit='unknown', branch='unknown', python_version='3.9.2')
>>> OtherNamedTuple = namedtuple("OtherNamedTuple", ["a", "b", "c"])
>>> other = OtherNamedTuple(a="unknown", b="unknown", c="3.9.2")
>>> other == program_info_a
True
```

Even though the OtherNamedTuple is bound to a different class name and has different field names (["a", "b", "c"] vs ["commit", "branch", "python_version"]), it's still possible for instances of OtherNamedTuple to compare equal to ProgramInfo. That's why other == program_info_a returns True—both program_info_a and other are comprised of the exact same number of elements in the same order. Keep in mind that this is the same behavior with plain tuple: ("unknown", "unknown", "3.9.2") == ("unknown", "unknown", "3.9.2") returns True. So, the behavior makes sense given that we're really just passing by tuples, but it's worth keeping in mind when using the namedtuple abstraction.

Its important to note that ProgramInfoClass (the variant we defined in code on page 42 without using namedtuple) doesn't support the same equality behavior. If we create two ProgramInfoClass instances with identical attributes and compare them, Python returns False because they are not considered equivalent:

```
>>> pi_a = ProgramInfoClass(commit="c", branch="b", python_version="3.9.2")
>>> pi_b = ProgramInfoClass(commit="c", branch="b", python_version="3.9.2")
>>> pi_a == pi_b
False
>>>
```

pi_a and pi_b are both ProgramInfoClass instances with identical values for their commit, branch, and python_version attributes. When you compare them by saying pi_a == pi_b, however, Python returns False. To be clear, pi_a and pi_b not being considered equivalent is the expected default behavior for custom Python classes and not necessarily surprising.[4] The point to be made, though, is that the ProgramInfo namedtuple version provides a helpful behavior by creating an equality method based on the ProgramInfo's attributes.

In the same way that ProgramInfo namedtuple instances with identical values are considered equal, ProgramInfo instances with identical values also hash to the same value:

```
>>> program_info_a = get_program_info()
>>> program_info_b = get_program_info()
>>> print(program_info_a)
ProgramInfo(commit='unknown', branch='unknown', python_version='3.9.2')
>>> print(program_info_b)
ProgramInfo(commit='unknown', branch='unknown', python_version='3.9.2')
>>> program_info_dict = {program_info_a: 'a'}
>>> program_info_dict[program_info_a]
'a'
>>> program_info_dict[program_info_b]
'a'
>>>
```

As before, two ProgramInfo namedtuple instances (program_info_a and program_info_b) are defined that have identical values for their attributes. The program_info_dict dictionary maps program_info_a to the value 'a'. Performing dictionary lookups on both program_info_a and program_info_b returns the same value of 'a'. In other words, both program_info_a and program_info_b hash to the same value, and are

4.   https://docs.python.org/3/reference/datamodel.html#object.__eq__

considered identical when put into a hash-based data structure like a dictionary.

As you might imagine, the same hashing behavior does not hold true with ProgramInfoClass instances that aren't based on namedtuple. ProgramInfoClass objects—even if they have identical attributes—do not hash the same and so they wind up in distinct dictionary keys:

```
>>> pi_a = ProgramInfoClass(commit="c", branch="b", python_version="3.9.2")
>>> pi_b = ProgramInfoClass(commit="c", branch="b", python_version="3.9.2")
>>> pi_dict = {pi_a: 'a'}
>>> pi_dict[pi_a]
'a'
>>> pi_dict[pi_b]
Traceback (most recent call last):
  File "<stdin>", line 1, in <module>
KeyError: <__main__.ProgramInfoClass object at 0x7ff52f5f43d0>
>>>
```

As before, both pi_a and pi_b are assigned to ProgramInfoClass instances with identical attributes. Notably, however, when pi_a is used as a dictionary key in pi_dict (mapped to a value of 'a'), pi_b doesn't hash to the same value (even though it has identical attributes). So, when you execute pi_dict[pi_b], a KeyError is raised indicating that pi_b cannot be found in the dictionary.

You've now explored namedtuple in detail: you've seen its debug string, learned how it prevents attribute reassignment, and investigated its equality and hashing behaviors. We'll close out with a few additional namedtuple tools.

Help Yourself to Extra namedtuple Conveniences

A few other conveniences with namedtuple are worth mentioning. In particular, classes returned by the namedtuple factory function include a number of other useful built-in methods and attributes.

To start, you can introspect a namedtuple at any time to find its field names using its _fields attribute:

```
>>> ProgramInfo._fields
('commit', 'branch', 'python_version')
```

Although underscore prefixes typically indicate private methods and attributes (as you'll learn more about in Maintaining Privacy in a Public World, on page 112), _fields is actually a documented public method for namedtuple.[5] Accessing _fields returns the names of the attributes defined on the given namedtuple: in

---

5.   https://docs.python.org/3/library/collections.html#collections.somenamedtuple._fields

this case `commit`, `branch`, and `python_version` from the `ProgramInfo` namedtuple we've been working with.

Another provided method worth highlighting is the `_as_dict` method. `_as_dict` allows you to convert a namedtuple instance into a dict at any time:

```
>>> pi = ProgramInfo(commit="c", branch="b", python_version="3.9.2")
>>> pi._as_dict()
{'commit': 'c', 'branch': 'b', 'python_version': '3.9.2'}
>>>
```

As with `_fields`, `_as_dict` is public despite the leading underscore that typically indicates privacy.[6] Calling `_as_dict()` returns a dictionary representation of the given namedtuple mapping its attribute names to their values.

You've learned a lot about namedtuple; let's wrap up with some details on how to integrate namedtuple with the mypy static analysis tool you learned about earlier.

Using namedtuple with mypy

You can add mypy type annotations to namedtuple using typing.NamedTuple.[a] For example, you can rewrite the ProgramInfo namedtuple that you first used in code on page 40 with type annotations:

```
from typing import NamedTuple

class ProgramInfo(NamedTuple):
    commit: str
    branch: str
    python_version: str

ProgramInfo(commit="c", branch="c", python_version="3.9.2")
```

The mypy type annotations—as you saw in Running mypy for Optimistic Type Checking, on page 23—help you detect and defeat bugs early by giving mypy a chance to statically analyze your code for problems ahead of time. In this case, you are explicitly informing mypy that commit, branch, and python_version attributes are all expected to be strings.

---

a. https://docs.python.org/3/library/typing.html#typing.NamedTuple

You have now completed our brief tour of the collections module: you can reduce boilerplate code using defaultdict, maintain tallies with Counter, and create tamper-resistant comparable objects using namedtuple. The collections module provides quite a few other utilities that you can peruse in Python's

---

6. https://docs.python.org/3/library/collections.html#collections.somenamedtuple._asdict

documentation.[7] In the next section we'll move on from data structures to file system access using tempfile.

Creating Temporary Workspaces with tempfile

The tempfile module allows you to create files and directories that are automatically deleted when you are done with them. As you'll see in this section, the tempfile module can be particularly useful when testing code that writes to the file system by allowing you to create new and isolated files and directories that are automatically cleaned up for you as the test ends.

tempfile has a number of convenience functions and classes, but you'll learn about two of the most useful in this section: NamedTemporaryFile and TemporaryDirectory.

Creating Temporary Files with NamedTemporaryFile

NamedTemporaryFile allows you to create a new file on the file system that is automatically deleted when you are done with it. Like other file operations, one of the most convenient ways to use NamedTemporaryFile is by using it in a with context manager (which ensures that file resources are properly cleaned up when you are finished):[8]

```
named_temporary_file.py
import os
from tempfile import NamedTemporaryFile

with NamedTemporaryFile() as tmp_f:
    print(tmp_f.name, os.path.exists(tmp_f.name))

print(tmp_f.name, os.path.exists(tmp_f.name))
```

If you run python3 named_temporary_file.py, you should receive output like the following:

```
/tmp/tmpy6yg9v95 True
/tmp/tmpy6yg9v95 False
```

In this example, NamedTemporaryFile is used in a with context manager to give us a handle on the newly created temporary file. Inside of the with context manager, the file exists, but when the with context manager exits, NamedTemporaryFile automatically deletes the file (even if an Exception was raised inside the with context manager). So, os.path.exists(tmp_f.name) returns True inside the with context manager and False after the context manager. Note that the path of the created NamedTemporaryFile

---

7. https://docs.python.org/3/library/collections.html
8. https://docs.python.org/3/tutorial/inputoutput.html#reading-and-writing-files

file will be different than the output shown earlier. (NamedTemporaryFile—by default—creates random file names in operating system dependent directories.)

NamedTemporaryFile Differences on Windows

On Windows, the file returned by NamedTemporaryFile cannot be opened again (for example, by another process that wants to manipulate the file). If you are developing primarily for Windows targets, it may be more convenient to use TemporaryDirectory to create a temporary directory that you can place files inside of (instead of trying to create individual files using NamedTemporaryFile). You will learn about TemporaryDirectory in the next section.

Consider the following example unittest TestCase that uses NamedTemporaryFile to exercise a function that writes a JSON data structure to a file:

test_write_people_json.py
```python
import json
import unittest
from tempfile import NamedTemporaryFile

def write_people_json(people, target_file_path):
    people_json = {"people": people}
    with open(target_file_path, mode="w") as f:
        json.dump(obj=people_json, fp=f)

class TestWritePeopleJSON(unittest.TestCase):
    def test_write_people_json(self):
        with NamedTemporaryFile() as tmp_f:
            write_people_json(
                people=["David", "Adaobi"],
                target_file_path=tmp_f.name,
            )

            expected_json = {"people": ["David", "Adaobi"]}
            actual_json = json.load(fp=tmp_f)
            self.assertEqual(expected_json, actual_json)

if __name__ == '__main__':
    unittest.main()
```

If you run this file using the unittest module like this:

```
python3 -m unittest test_write_people_json.py
```

you should see output like the following:

```
.
----------------------------------------------------------------------
Ran 1 test in 0.003s

OK
```

test_write_people_json.py defines a function named write_people_json. write_people_json accepts two arguments: people and target_file_path. write_people_json constructs a dictionary mapping the key "people" to the supplied value of people. The file at target_file_path is opened for writing (mode="w"), and the json module function dump is used to write a JSON representation of the previously created dictionary into target_file_path.

A unittest TestCase subclass named TestWritePeopleJSON defines a single test method named test_write_people_json. test_write_people_json uses NamedTemporaryFile to create a temporary file object bound to the variable named tmp_f. The absolute path to the new temporary file is passed to write_people_json using the .name attribute of tmp_f. Then, the test reads the JSON contents of tmp_f using json.load to confirm that the expected data structure was written to the file.

Running python3 -m unittest test_write_people_json.py executes the test. The single dot in the output represents that a test passed. Indeed, the end of the unittest output indicates that one test passed. Notably, after the python3 -m unittest test_write_people_json.py completes, no dangling files are left on the file system. You just successfully created a temporary file for a test to use, and that file was automatically deleted for you.

In the next section, you'll learn about a tempfile utility that allows you to create directories that—like the files generated by NamedTemporaryFile—are automatically deleted for you.

Using TemporaryDirectory

The tempfile module provides the TemporaryDirectory function for creating directories that are automatically deleted for you. To see how this works, consider the following example using TemporaryDirectory:

```
temporary_directory.py
import os
from tempfile import TemporaryDirectory

with TemporaryDirectory() as tmp_d_path:
    print(tmp_d_path, os.path.isdir(tmp_d_path))

    example_txt_path = os.path.join(tmp_d_path, "example.txt")
    with open(example_txt_path, mode="w") as f:
        f.write("example contents")
    print(example_txt_path, os.path.exists(example_txt_path))

print(tmp_d_path, os.path.isdir(tmp_d_path))
print(example_txt_path, os.path.exists(example_txt_path))
```

If you run python3 temporary_directory.py, you should receive output like the following:

```
/tmp/tmppwnkhh7e True
/tmp/tmppwnkhh7e/example.txt True
/tmp/tmppwnkhh7e False
/tmp/tmppwnkhh7e/example.txt False
```

Note that the temporary directory created on your file system will have a different path than the one generated in the example. Using TemporaryDirectory as a context manager allows us to bind the path of the newly created temporary directory to the variable tmp_d_path. Printing out tmp_d_path we see where the temporary directory is on the file system, and calling os.path.isdir verifies that the directory indeed exists. Next, we place a file named example.txt into the directory using the built-in open method and write some contents in it. We use os.path.exists to verify that this file indeed exists—indeed the output shows True: the file example.txt exists in our temporary directory.

Semantic Differences Between NamedTemporaryFile and TemporaryDirectory

 You may have noticed that the TemporaryDirectory interface is slightly different than NamedTemporaryFile. The TemporaryDirectory's with context manager returns a string with the path to the created directory, whereas the NamedTemporaryFile context manager returns a file object whose name attribute can be used to find the full path to the file.

After the with context manager exits (even if an exception was somehow raised in its body), the directory and all of its contents are deleted. temporary_directory.py confirms this because os.path.isdir returns False after the with statement and the example.txt file also no longer exists.

TemporaryDirectory allows you to create temporary workspaces that you can place files in using Python's built-in open function. It can be especially helpful when writing tests or trying out procedures that need to create several files all grouped together in a single directory.

In the next section we'll move beyond the file system and learn how to invoke external programs using Python's subprocess module.

Calling Other Programs with subprocess

You can use the subprocess standard library module to invoke other command line programs available on your system and process their results in Python. You might find the subprocess useful if, for example, you want to call a program like git from inside Python to learn about the current state of your version controlled project. Indeed, some examples in this section will combine subprocess and git to do just that.

Note, if you don't have git installed on your machine or are not currently in a directory with a git repository, some of the following examples may not successfully execute on your computer. You can download git if you like,[9] but it's also OK to just follow along with the examples here so you get a sense of the abilities of the subprocess module (you don't need any special git knowledge).

You can use subprocess with git to retrieve the name of the current git branch you are on:

```
>>> import subprocess
>>> command = ["git", "branch", "--show-current"]
>>> result = subprocess.run(command, capture_output=True)
>>> result.returncode
0
>>> result.stdout
b'main\n'
>>> result.stdout.decode("utf-8").strip()
'main'
>>>
```

In the preceding example, you call subprocess.run with two arguments. The first argument (command) is a list of strings specifying the command line program you want to run. In general, you can think of Python as telling the operating system to execute as if there were spaces separating them. In other words ["git", "branch", "--show-current"] is roughly translated to git branch --show-current and executed by the operating system. (Python automatically handles any necessary escaping and quoting for you. This escaping and quoting can be helpful if, for example, one of the arguments in your list is a file name with a space in it.)

The second argument capture_output flag instructs Python to record stdout and stderr and make them available to you in the CompletedProcess object[10] returned by subprocess.run. In the preceding example, the result variable is bound to the CompletedProcess object. result.returncode indicates that the git command you ran exited with a 0 code. Accessing result.stdout returns bytes with the output of the underlying git command we ran. Decoding the bytes as utf-8[11] and calling strip[12] to remove the trailing newline \n character leaves us with a Python string indicating my current branch name: 'main'.

---

9. https://git-scm.com
10. https://docs.python.org/3/library/subprocess.html#subprocess.CompletedProcess
11. https://en.wikipedia.org/wiki/UTF-8
12. https://docs.python.org/3/library/stdtypes.html#str.strip

Let subprocess.run Automatically Decode bytes for You

On Python 3.7 or higher, you can pass text=True to subprocess.run. subprocess.run will then automatically coerce the resulting bytes in stdout and stderr to strings and save you from having to call decode on the bytes yourself.

So far, we've only worked with an example where the underlying command we called worked. What happens if the underlying command failed and returned a non-0 returncode?

Handling Exceptional Cases with subprocess

Python can automatically raise an exception for you if the underlying command didn't exit with a returncode of 0. If you pass check=True to subprocess.run, it will raise an Exception if the underlying command fails:

```
>>> import subprocess
>>> subprocess.run(["git", "oops"], check=True)
git: 'oops' is not a git command. See 'git --help'.

The most similar command is
    notes
Traceback (most recent call last):
  File "<stdin>", line 1, in <module>
  File "/usr/local/lib/python3.9/subprocess.py", line 528, in run
    raise CalledProcessError(retcode, process.args,
subprocess.CalledProcessError: Command '['git', 'oops']' returned
non-zero exit status 1.
>>>
```

git does not support a subcommand named oops, so when you try to execute git oops, git complains and returns a non-0 returncode. By including the check=True argument in your subprocess.run call, Python automatically raises a CalledProcessError exception for you indicating the failure. This CalledProcessError exception can be useful if you want your program to exit or otherwise fail if the underlying command you call doesn't work.

Timing Out Commands Run By subprocess

You can also instruct subprocess to automatically kill the underlying command if it has not completed after a certain amount of time using the timeout argument to subprocess.run:

```
>>> import subprocess
>>> subprocess.run(["sleep", "2"], timeout=1)
Traceback (most recent call last):
  File "<stdin>", line 1, in <module>
  File "/usr/local/lib/python3.9/subprocess.py", line 507, in run
```

```
    stdout, stderr = process.communicate(input, timeout=timeout)
  File "/usr/local/lib/python3.9/subprocess.py", line 1134, in communicate
    stdout, stderr = self._communicate(input, endtime, timeout)
  File "/usr/local/lib/python3.9/subprocess.py", line 2007, in _communicate
    self.wait(timeout=self._remaining_time(endtime))
  File "/usr/local/lib/python3.9/subprocess.py", line 1189, in wait
    return self._wait(timeout=timeout)
  File "/usr/local/lib/python3.9/subprocess.py", line 1911, in _wait
    raise TimeoutExpired(self.args, timeout)
subprocess.TimeoutExpired: Command '['sleep', '2']' timed out after
0.9996613000002981 seconds
>>>
```

By passing the timeout=1 argument to subprocess.run, you are instructing subpro-cess.run to raise a TimeoutExpired exception after approximately one second has passed and the underlying command hasn't completed.[13] Since the sleep 2 command just waits for two seconds, it should never complete in one second and, indeed, you see a TimeoutExpired exception raised in the preceding output. Notably—as you may have surmised from the output—the timeout operation is made on a best effort basis and may be above or below the timeout value you request. In this case, for example, it was actually just under one second before the TimeoutExpired exception was raised.

You've now seen how to call external programs, handle errors they might return, and kill them if they are taking too long. Next, you'll learn how you can invoke programs that might need to have data sent to them over stdin.

Passing Input to External Programs with subprocess

Sometimes, it's useful to pass input to command line programs via stdin—either because the underlying program requires it, or you have a significant amount of data that you don't want to load into RAM.

Use the input Argument to Pass bytes to stdin

For simple cases when you want to pass data to the stdin of a program, you can use the input argument to subprocess.run. For example, you can search a sequence of input bytes with grep:

```
>>> import subprocess
>>> to_grep = b"Alpha\nBeta\nGamma"
>>> command = ["grep", "eta"]
>>> result = subprocess.run(command, input=to_grep, capture_output=True)
>>> result.stdout
b'Beta\n'
>>>
```

---

13. https://docs.python.org/3/library/subprocess.html#subprocess.TimeoutExpired

In this example, we define an input sequence of bytes that we want to grep through: b"Alpha\nBeta\nGamma". Next, we define our grep command as grep eta—we are searching for lines in the input that contain eta. Using the input argument to subprocess.run, we pass our to_grep bytes to our grep eta command as stdin. grep responds that it found one matching line b'Beta'\n. You have successfully passed stdin to a child program using subprocess!

Notably, when you use the input argument to subprocess.run you need all the data you want to pass as stdin to be loaded into your application's RAM. What if the data you wanted to pass through stdin was large—large enough, for example, that you wouldn't want to store it in the RAM of your Python application?

Use the stdin Argument to Pass Data Stored in Files to stdin

It turns out that subprocess.run also supports an argument besides input for passing values to stdin. subprocess.run actually includes an argument named stdin, which can accept file objects like those produced by the built-in open command. That was a lot to unpack, but let's try with an example where we pass the contents of a file to grep:

subprocess_with_stdin.py
```python
import subprocess

with open("example.txt", mode="w") as f:
    contents = "example\ntext\nfile"
    f.write(contents)

with open("example.txt", mode="r") as f:
    result = subprocess.run(
        ["grep", "l"], stdin=f, capture_output=True, check=True
    )

stdout_str = result.stdout.decode("utf-8").strip()
print(stdout_str)
```

In the preceding example, the file example.txt is created and has the strings example, text, and file written into it with each word on its own line. Then, example.txt is opened for reading (mode="r") and its file object[14] bound to f is passed as the value for subprocess.run's stdin argument. The command in subprocess.run is ["grep", "l"], which translates roughly to, "find lines in the input that include l in them." The result of the subprocess.run call is bound to result, and the captured stdout value is decoded from bytes into a string, stripped of its trailing newline, and printed.

If you run python3 subprocess_with_stdin.py, you should see output like this:

---

14. https://docs.python.org/3/glossary.html#term-file-object

‹ example
  file

grep has found all the lines in our file which had l in them, and the output indicates this. Importantly, you were able to pass stdin to grep without loading the entire contents of example.txt into RAM, which might be problematic if you are working with large files. In this example, example.txt was a file of trivial size, but you can imagine working with files much larger than example.txt.

The stdout and stderr arguments to subprocess.run[15] also support being passed as file objects. You can use file objects in place of the pipes[16] and redirects[17] you may be more familiar with from traditional shells. As you just learned about in Creating Temporary Workspaces with tempfile, on page 47, you can even take advantage of NamedTempfile and TemporaryDirectory to use as short-lived workspaces for your endeavors with subprocess.

In this section, you learned how to dispatch commands to the underlying operating system. In the next section, you'll learn how to use the sqlite3 standard library module to gain access to another powerful tool: sqlite.

Using Python's Built-In Database with sqlite3

A fully featured SQL database called SQLite comes bundled with your Python programming language install. In case you haven't used SQLite before, it's a SQL database engine that stores all your table and row data in a single file. SQLite pervades software today: it comes with every Android and iOS phone, all the major web browsers, inside PHP, all Macs, and so forth.[18]

You can use Python's sqlite3 standard library module to create a SQLite database, connect to it, and write and read contents from it.

You can use SQLite in a lot of ways—it's fast and consumes very little RAM. I've seen it used when, for example, a team needed to perform membership tests on hundreds of thousands of elements without loading all those entries into RAM. (In practice, they had hundreds of thousands of latitude/longitude pairs and wanted to see if a random latitude/longitude pair was one of the existing pairs.) The entries were kept in a SQLite database, and membership tests were performed by querying the SQLite database—the application used very minimal amount of RAM and accomplished its goals without any external database servers or excess state.

---

15. https://docs.python.org/3/library/subprocess.html#subprocess.run
16. https://en.wikipedia.org/wiki/Pipeline_%28Unix%29
17. https://en.wikipedia.org/wiki/Redirection_(computing)
18. https://sqlite.org/mostdeployed.html

What Does SQLite Do Well?

SQLite pervades software for good reason: its backing file format is fully backward compatible and cross platform, and SQLite is an exceptionally well-tested application. If you give someone a SQLite file, they will be able to open it and seek through its contents efficiently (no matter how big they might be). SQLite—effectively—gives you a file that you can write to transactionally without worrying about concurrency bugs, operating system idiosyncrasies, network latency, power failures, or data corruption. You might want to use SQLite if you have a large amount of row-based data to store, need several distinct processes to cooperatively and simultaneously read and write to a single file location, or need a stable file format to save and transmit application state in.

In a similar spirit to a list of allowed latitude/longitude pairs, let's try using the sqlite3 module to store an allowlist of usernames.

Creating a SQLite Database

To create a SQLite database you can call the connect function from the sqlite3 standard library module:

```
>>> import sqlite3
>>> connection = sqlite3.connect("example.db")
```

Calling the connect function creates a SQLite database file with the given name and returns a Connection object[19] that you can use to interact with the database. If you look in your current working directory you should see that a file named example.db has appeared. The example.db file contains your (currently empty) database. You can delete it at anytime if you want to wash your hands of it and start over as you proceed through this section.

One handy feature of the connect function is that you can call it repeatedly with the same database name, and it will gracefully handle if the example.db file already exists; only one backing database file will ever appear and you get no errors.

```
>>> import sqlite3
>>> connection = sqlite3.connect("example.db")
>>> connection = sqlite3.connect("example.db")
>>> connection = sqlite3.connect("example.db")
```

---

19. https://docs.python.org/3/library/sqlite3.html#sqlite3.Connection

Calling connect("example.db") three times does not cause any exceptions to be raised, and if you inspect your working directory you'll see that only one example.db file exists.

> ### In Memory sqlite Database
>
> SQLite also supports operating a database exclusively in RAM. If you pass the special string ":memory:" to sqlite3.connect (for example, sqlite3.connect(":memory:")), you'll get a connection to a unique database that only exists in RAM.
>
> Unlike the file-based mode we've used so far, if you call sqlite3.connect(":memory:") repeatedly, you'll get pointers to distinct SQLite databases. Also, if you discard the connection to the database or exit your Python process, the database will effectively disappear. Using the ":memory:" database can be helpful as a temporary sandbox if you want to try something out in SQLite.

Now that you've successfully created a SQLite database and connected to it, let's move on to adding data to it.

Adding Data to a SQLite Database

To add data to a SQLite database, you use a Connection object (like the one you've just created) in concert with a Cursor object.[20]

Let's consider an example where we connect to a database named example.db, create a table named allowed, and insert two rows into that table:

```
add_sqlite_data.py
import contextlib
import sqlite3


with sqlite3.connect("example.db") as connection:
    with contextlib.closing(connection.cursor()) as cursor:
        cursor.execute("CREATE TABLE IF NOT EXISTS allowed (name text)")
        cursor.execute("INSERT INTO allowed values ('Arthur')")
        cursor.execute("INSERT INTO allowed values ('Lancelot')")
        cursor.execute("SELECT name from allowed")
        print(cursor.fetchall())
```

If you run python3 add_sqlite_data.py, you'll see the following output:

```
[('Arthur',), ('Lancelot',)]
```

What exactly happened? Let's break it down. First, a connection is opened to example.db using a with context manager on line 5. The with context manager

---

20. https://docs.python.org/3/library/sqlite3.html#sqlite3.Cursor

ensures that the connection to the database is cleaned up and closed even if an exception is raised inside of the with block. The with context manager also ensures that any modifications made to database tables and rows inside the with block are committed at the end of the block. If there is an exception, all the changes to the database are rolled back. In short, you can think of the connection with block as: cleanly try to do all of the below contents, but if there is any problem cleanly abort all of it.

What Are Commits and Rollbacks?

SQL databases—like SQLite—support operations called transactions. Briefly, a transaction is a series of operations (e.g., adding Arthur and Lancelot rows to the allowed tables) that are grouped together in an all-or-nothing fashion. If an error occurs while the transaction is running (for example, your computer is suddenly shut down or the database raises an error because the input is invalid), the whole transaction aborts and any of the partially completed changes are rolled back. If nothing goes wrong, however, the transaction is committed and all the changes stick. If you want to learn more about SQL semantics including transactions, commits, and rollbacks, the "Database Transaction" Wikipedia entry is a great intro.[21]

After creating the connection to example.db, line 6 creates a second object called cursor. The cursor object is the actual object that you use to send commands to the database. As with the database connection itself, its a good practice to use a with context manager to ensure that the cursor is cleaned up (via its close() method)[22] when the with block ends. To have the close method called automatically at the end of cursor's with block, we use the contextlib.closing helper function.[23]

In case you are wondering what the purpose of the Cursor object is, you are not alone—many people in this linked Stack Overflow question have wondered the same.[24] For the most part, you can just think of the Cursor as a way for you to fetch rows and send other operations to the database. Unfortunately, Cursor objects in Python's sqlite3 module do not quite match the traditional definition of a SQL database cursor—something that can be confusing for

---

21. https://en.wikipedia.org/wiki/Database_transaction
22. https://docs.python.org/3/library/sqlite3.html#sqlite3.Cursor.close
23. https://docs.python.org/3/library/contextlib.html#contextlib.closing
24. https://stackoverflow.com/q/6318126

developers with SQL backgrounds.[25] In general, it's enough for you to understand sqlite3 Cursor object just as an intermediate abstraction to fetch rows and perform operations.

At this point, you've created a Connection object named connection and a Cursor object named cursor off of connection. Both connection and cursor will be automatically closed and cleaned up for you because you've used with context managers. Now that all the prep work is done, you can apply some SQL.

To issue a command to the database, you call cursor.execute() with the given SQL command you'd like to run. In the preceding example, you ran four statements starting on line 7:

1. cursor.execute("CREATE TABLE IF NOT EXISTS allowed (name text)")
2. cursor.execute("INSERT INTO allowed values ('Arthur')")
3. cursor.execute("INSERT INTO allowed values ('Lancelot')")
4. cursor.execute("SELECT name from allowed")

The first statement creates a new SQL table named allowed that has a single column called name which stores text data. The IF NOT EXISTS ensures that no error is raised if the allowed table already exists (something that might happen if, for example, you run add_sqlite_data.py multiple times).

Statements 2 and 3 each add one row to the allowed table. Statement 2 adds a row with a user named Arthur. Statement 3 adds a row with a user named Lancelot.

The fourth statement reads these two new rows back out using a SELECT statement. Calling cursor.fetchall() retrieves the output from the last SQL statement executed (in this case the SELECT) and returns a list of Row objects:[26] [('Arthur',), ('Lancelot',)].

At this point, you've successfully connected to a sqlite database, created a table, inserted rows into that table, and read them back out. You'll have a file named example.db in your current working directory with these new contents, and that data will persist, even if you exit Python. As long as that file is still around, the data is still there.

In the last section of the chapter, we'll move to a part of the standard library that doesn't help you build new tools, but lets you inspect what you've run to see exactly how it is executing and performing.

---

25. http://en.wikipedia.org/wiki/Cursor_%28databases%29
26. https://docs.python.org/3/library/sqlite3.html#sqlite3.Row

Profiling Python Code with cProfile

Finding bottlenecks in your code can help you write more performant scripts and procedures. Python's standard library includes a profiling module named cProfile to help you find where your program is spending its time; you'll learn about cProfile in this section.

In general, to use cProfile you can do the following:

1. Enable a profiler and run the code you'd like to profile (disabling the profiler when you are done).

2. Investigate the Stats produced by the profiling session.[27]

Let's try this out with an example. cprofile_example.py profiles the function named a and writes the Stats to a file named example.stats:

cprofile_example.py
```
import cProfile

def a():
    b()
    b()

def b():
    for i in range(250000):
        pass

profiler = cProfile.Profile()
profiler.enable()

a()

profiler.disable()
profiler.dump_stats("example.stats")
```

cprofile_example.py defines two functions: a and b. All a does is call b twice, and all b does is iterate over 250,000 numbers. A profiling session is started by calling enable() on a cProfile.Profile instance bound to profiler. Then function a is called once, and the profiling session is ended by calling profiler.disable(). Finally, the Stats of the profiling session are written out to a file named example.stats using the dump_stats method on the cProfile.Profile instance.

If you run cprofile_example.py (e.g. python3 cprofile_example.py), you should see a file example.stats appear in your current working directory. You've now completed

---

27. https://docs.python.org/3/library/profile.html#pstats.Stats

step 1: you've profiled some code you were interested in and generated some Stats to investigate.

Next, let's investigate the Stats held in example.stats using a Python interactive console. After you import the pstats standard library module, you can start working with your generated profiling information in example.stats using pstats.Stats:

```
>>> import pstats
>>> stats = pstats.Stats("example.stats")
>>> stats.print_stats()
Sat Dec 12 17:34:58 2020    example.stats

        4 function calls in 0.014 seconds

   Random listing order was used

   ncalls  tottime  percall  cumtime  percall filename:lineno(function)
        1    0.000    0.000    0.014    0.014 cprofile_example.py:3(a)
        2    0.014    0.007    0.014    0.007 cprofile_example.py:7(b)
        1    0.000    0.000    0.000    0.000 {method 'disable' of
        '_lsprof.Profiler' objects}


<pstats.Stats object at 0x1011e41f0>
>>>
```

After creating a Stats instance (bound to the variable named stats), you are able to print out stats about the profiling information using the print_stats method. When you run print_stats(), you see output that indicates what functions were called and for how long. The columns (ncalls, tottime, percall, etc.) are the most important part of the output to understand, the meaning of each column is described in the table shown on page 62.

With those column descriptions in mind, you can now understand the output that describes how functions a and b were called:

```
ncalls  tottime  percall  cumtime  percall filename:lineno(function)
     1    0.000    0.000    0.014    0.014 cprofile_example.py:3(a)
     2    0.014    0.007    0.014    0.007 cprofile_example.py:7(b)
```

Function a was called one time and spent tottime of 0.000 seconds running its own code. Evidently, it must have spent most of its runtime in subfunctions: it spent a cumulative total of 0.014 cumtime seconds in itself and subfunctions. Recall, from the code on page 60, that function a just calls function b twice. Indeed, on the next line of output we see two total calls for function b. b spent 0.014 totime executing its own code and 0.014 cumtime executing its own code and subfunctions (notably b does not have any subfunctions so the times are equivalent).

Column	Description
ncalls	Number of times function was called. (It's not shown in our example output, but if you ever see two numbers separated by a slash, the second number is the total number of calls and the first number is the number of nonrecursive calls.)
tottime	Amount of time spent in the function (not counting any time spent in subfunctions).
percall	tottime / ncalls
cumtime	All the time spent in the function and subfunctions.
percall	Note that percall appears twice. This second time it represents cumtime / primitive calls (where primitive calls are nonrecursive calls to the given function).
filename:lineno(function)	Indicates the function that was called and where it is defined.

The final entry of the output is an artifact of using cProfile itself:

```
1    0.000    0.000    0.000    0.000 {method 'disable' of
'_lsprof.Profiler' objects}
```

It's safe for us to just ignore this line—it's an artifact of us ending our profiling session by calling profiler.disable().

You now have a handle on the standard output of print_stats(). In the real world when you profile code, you are likely to see many more lines of output from print_stats() (because your programs will inevitably be more complicated than cprofile_example.py). To work with these larger output sets, you'll need to be able to sort and filter the print_stats() output to quickly identify hotspots. There are many ways to perform this sorting and filtering, but next we'll explore a few helpful patterns to get you started.

Digging Deeper into pstat.Stats

Continuing to examine the example.stats you generated earlier, the fastest way to get started with almost any amount of output is to sort by cumtime (to find which function calls take a long time to return). You can sort by cumtime and restrict the output to the top n lines by using sort_stats in combination with print_stats(n):

```
>>> import pstats
>>> stats = pstats.Stats("example.stats")
>>> stats.sort_stats("cumtime").print_stats(2)

Sat Dec 12 17:34:58 2020    example.stats
         4 function calls in 0.014 seconds

   Ordered by: cumulative time
   List reduced from 3 to 2 due to restriction <2>

   ncalls  tottime  percall  cumtime  percall filename:lineno(function)
        1    0.000    0.000    0.014    0.014 cprofile_example.py:3(a)
        2    0.014    0.007    0.014    0.007 cprofile_example.py:7(b)

<pstats.Stats object at 0x101241100>
>>>
```

In our toy example, we still see the same entries for functions a and b (and indeed still in the same order as before), but we've filtered out the third entry by passing 2 to print_stats, as in, "limit the outputted stats to two lines."

When profiling more significant code, you'll have a list of hundreds or thousands of lines to look through—many with significantly large values for cumtime. You'll want to look at the top candidate functions by saying sort_stats("cumtime") and then dig in and look a little closer at individual entries. Two of the most useful methods for this kind of analysis are print_callees and print_callers to see who called whom. For example, to see what functions were invoked by a, you can use print_callees:

```
>>> import pstats
>>> stats = pstats.Stats("example.stats")
>>> stats.print_callees("cprofile_example.py:3")  # :3 is for line 3

   Random listing order was used
   List reduced from 3 to 1 due to restriction <'cprofile_example.py:3'>

Function                      called...
                                  ncalls  tottime  cumtime
cprofile_example.py:3(a)  ->       2    0.014    0.014  cprofile_exam
ple.py:7(b)

<pstats.Stats object at 0x1012410d0>
>>>
```

The print_callees method takes one or more so-called restriction arguments. In this case, the supplied restriction was "cprofile_example.py:3" (a.k.a. the location of the definition of function a on line 3). The output then shows that function a called function b two times for 0.014 tottime and 0.014 cumtime. (Note that this book's width is limited to 76 characters, so normally there would not be a line break in the middle of cprofile_example.py:7(b).)

It's often helpful to find a function that has a large amount of cumtime using sort_stats("cumtime"), and then dig in and look at its callees by saying print_callees to see where, in turn, that function wound up spending time. You can also perform the inverse, and look up a function's callers. This can be helpful if, for example, you have a function that is taking a lot of time, but you don't know who is calling it. To look at a function's callers, you use the print_callers function:

```
>>> import pstats
>>> stats = pstats.Stats("example.stats")
>>> stats.print_callers("cprofile_example.py:7")

   Random listing order was used
   List reduced from 3 to 1 due to restriction <'cprofile_example.py:7'>

Function                     was called by...
                                 ncalls  tottime  cumtime
cprofile_example.py:7(b)    <-        2    0.014    0.014  cprofile_exam
ple.py:3(a)

<pstats.Stats object at 0x1012410d0>
>>>
```

In this case, we looked for the callers of "cprofile_example.py:7" (a.k.a. function b). The printed stats indicated that function b was called two times by function a, and the corresponding timing stats also outputted.

At this point, you have a good grasp of the basics of the cProfile standard library module. You understand the outputted columns and how to peruse the rows of outputs using sorting and caller/callee printing techniques. As you practice with cProfile more, you'll become comfortable with it and able to use it to quickly find performance problems and bottlenecks in your code. The cProfile documentation is a great place to continue learning.[28]

Can I Visualize cProfile Stats Graphically?

 Yes, it's possible to visualize the results of a cProfile profiling session graphically. SnakeViz, for example, will interatively render a profiling output file (like the example.stats file you've been working with) in your web browser.[29] SnakeViz's visualization can make it easier to explore results and find hotspots in your programs.

28. https://docs.python.org/3/library/profile.html#pstats.Stats.sort_stats
29. https://jiffyclub.github.io/snakeviz/

Wrapping Up

You've now completed a tour of selections from Python's standard library: you used collections.defaultdict and collections.namedtuple to level up your usage of the built-in types tuple and dict, created temporary workspaces using tempfile, delegated calls to other programs with subprocess, wrote SQL from within Python with sqlite3, and even profiled your code with cProfile. You've covered a lot of ground!

You are well prepared to move on to another important subject in any programming language: concurrency. In the next chapter, we'll focus on how to run Python code concurrently with its provided concurrency tools.

## CHAPTER 3

Ramping Up with Concurrent Code

It's a chilly autumn morning, and several hundred runners are lined up behind the starting line. The runners are excited to begin the 10-kilometer race, and I'm one of them.

I've never won a race. It's not for lack of trying—I've run plenty of races over varying distances. But I've never won.

Sometimes I'll start a race off at a good pace and then get a stitch in my side and slow down. I usually feel like I'm running fast, but then I'll be halfway through a race only to see a parent pushing a child in a stroller and chatting on a cell phone pass me. I prepare for the race by jogging the distance on my own ahead of time. But, whatever I do, there's always someone that day who is faster.

I compensate for my losing streak by entering more races. I don't win any of those either.

Am I a slow runner? Yes. Does this have anything to do with Python? Yes.

Python runs your programs slowly. There, I said it! Maybe you already suspected as much, maybe you only feared as much, but now you know. Python runs slow. Programs written in Go, Java, Rust, or other languages often beat Python in straight line races.

In real life, I make up for not winning races by running more races. It can be the same with Python.

Running multiple Python programs concurrently can help you arrive at your desired outcome, when just one lone Python program wouldn't cut it. Enter the world of concurrency.

In this chapter, you will learn about concurrency primitives in Python including threads and processes and the global interpreter lock.

In the previous chapter, you got a tour of some of the finer components of the Python standard library. After you read this chapter, you will be able to run those components under threads and processes and understand how each can help you run more of your code at the same time.

Approach Concurrency with Caution

Running your code concurrently sounds appealing—who doesn't want to run more code? Unfortunately, running code concurrently can create problems that you didn't realize even existed. Before diving into concurrency, we'll start this chapter with a brief forewarning.

One class of problems caused by concurrency are called race conditions. In a classic race condition example, two concurrent banking operations accidentally allow a customer to overdraw his bank account:

1. Customer David has $8 in his bank account.
2. Process A reads David's balance of $8.
3. Process B reads David's balance of $8.
4. Process A allows David to withdraw $6.
5. Process A updates David's balance to $8 - $6 = $2.
6. Process A ends.
7. Process B allows David to withdraw $7.
8. Process B updates David's balance to $8 - $7 = $1.
9. Process B ends.

Oops! David only has $8, but was able to withdraw a total of $6 + $7 = $13. David's balance is now $1, but it should be -$5!

Why did the banking software allow David to overdraw his account? The problem occurred at step 3 when process B read David's balance as $8 without realizing process A was about to reduce David's balance.

If process A and process B didn't run at the same time, David would not have been able to overdraw his account:

1. Customer David has $8 in his bank account.
2. Process A reads David's balance of $8.
3. Process A allows David to withdraw $6.
4. Process A updates David's balance to $8 - $6 = $2.
5. Process A ends.
6. Process B reads David's balance of $2.
7. Process B raises an error when David tries to withdraw $7.
8. Process B ends.

When Process B runs strictly after Process A, David's balance is not overdrawn, and all is well in the world.

Beyond race conditions, another potential problem associated with concurrency (among others) are deadlocks.

Deadlocks occur when multiple concurrent programs wait on each other indefinitely. Deadlocks typically occur when programs make use of a tool called locks. Locks are a coordination tool that allow programs to declare that a certain resource is in use by one program and shouldn't be accessed by another.

Let's illustrate deadlock with an example involving two simultaneous transfers between bank accounts owned by David and Margaret.

1. Process A initiates a transfer of $2 from David → Margaret.
2. Process B initiates a transfer of $4 from Margaret → David.
3. Process A locks David's account (to protect its balance from being corrupted).
4. Process B locks Margaret's account.
5. Process A tries to acquire a lock on Margaret's account.
6. Process B tries to acquire a lock on David's account.
7. Process A waits...Process B already has a lock on Margaret's account.
8. Process B waits...Process A already has a lock on David's account.

Process A and Process B try to lock David's and Margaret's account to ensure that no other Processes are modifying the underlying accounts at the same time. Locking the accounts, ostensibly, helps ensure that the bank account data is accessed in a controlled way that prevents bank account balances from being corrupted by race conditions. Unfortunately, Processes A and B are stuck blocking and endlessly wait for each other. Process A holds a lock on David's account, that Process B wants. Process B holds a lock on Margaret's account that Process A wants. Neither can proceed: the processes are stuck waiting on each other and the transfers will never go through.

The locks seemed like a good idea, but a subtle timing issue means that the banking software may fail to do its job and frustrate its users.

As we've seen with the race condition and deadlock examples, introducing concurrency to your program can create problems that you never thought existed. So, be careful and only consider adding concurrency if absolutely necessary.

In the rest of this chapter, we'll examine the tools Python provides for writing concurrent code and see how to avoid these dangers.

Meet Threads and Processes

Python provides two keystone standard library modules that allow you to run code concurrently:

1. threading
2. multiprocessing

The threading module provides the Thread object for running code with threads and the multiprocessing module provides the Process object for running code with processes.

What Are Threads and Processes?

 Threads and processes are abstractions provided by your operating system that allow you to run code. In general, processes are independent sequences of execution with their own dedicated memory space. Threads, by contrast, live within a process. One or more threads can run within a given parent process. Threads share memory with each other and the parent process.

The following table summarizes some of the key differences between threads and processes in Python:

Module	Paradigm	Object	Share Memory?	Restricted by GIL?
threading	threads	Thread	Yes	Yes
multiprocessing	processes	Process	No	No

In later sections, we'll discuss the last two columns: memory sharing and the effects of something called the GIL on Thread and Process objects. First, we'll focus how to use Thread and Process objects to run code concurrently.

Using concurrent.futures to Run Code Concurrently

The concurrent.futures module provides a unified high-level interface over both Thread and Process objects (so you don't have to use the low-level interfaces in threading and process).

While concurrent.futures may not be able to run code concurrently in all the ways that you'd expect based on reading the underlying threading and multiprocessing modules, concurrent.futures is a great place to start. It exposes an approachable interface for executing code under threads and processes and gives you the power to run code concurrently without needing to get into the grittiest details of concurrent programming. If you can write a function in Python, you can use concurrent.futures.

The two most important classes provided by concurrent.futures are:

```
concurrent.futures.ThreadPoolExecutor
concurrent.futures.ProcessPoolExecutor
```

ThreadPoolExecutor and ProcessPoolExecutor allow you to run code and retrieve outputs using Thread objects and Process objects, respectively. ThreadPoolExecutor and ProcessPoolExecutor hide the details about the underlying Thread and Process so that you can write clean and clear code. Additionally, since the two classes expose virtually identical interfaces, you can quickly switch strategies between threads and processes with little additional work.

Let's consider an example that uses ProcessPoolExecutor to perform a series of multiplications:

```
process_pool_executor.py
import concurrent.futures

def multiply(a, b):
    value = a * b
    print(f"{a} * {b} = {value}")

if __name__ == "__main__":
    with concurrent.futures.ProcessPoolExecutor() as executor:
        for i in range(5):
            executor.submit(multiply, a=i, b=i)
```

If you run python3 process_pool_executor.py, you should see output roughly like the following:

```
0 * 0 = 0
2 * 2 = 4
1 * 1 = 1
4 * 4 = 16
3 * 3 = 9
```

Let's break down what is happening:

- import concurrent.futures makes the concurrent.futures module available to our code.

- A function named multiply is defined that multiplies its inputs a and b together and prints the result.

- The if __name__ == "__main__" block is entered because process_pool_executor.py is the file you ran by saying python3 process_pool_executor.py (and thus has its __name__ set to "__main__").[1]

---

1. https://stackoverflow.com/a/419189

- A with statement is used to create a ProcessPoolExecutor named executor. The with statement ensures that all the jobs submitted to the executor are completed before the with statement closes and resources are cleaned up afterward.

- A for loop submits five multiplication jobs to executor (0 * 0, 1 * 1, 2 * 2, 3 * 3, and 4 * 4).

- The output shows the results of the five multiplications. Importantly, the results you receive may not be output in the order shown in this book. The jobs are submitted to the executor, and the executor handles running them—not necessarily in the sequence they were submitted in.

By using ProcessPoolExecutor, Python ultimately used Process objects to run the multiplication jobs. We could just as easily swapped out ProcessPoolExecutor with ThreadPoolExecutor, and the results would have been the same. ProcessPoolExecutor and ThreadPoolExecutor implement the same interface, they just dispatch to different lower-level machinery: Process objects or Thread objects.

Processing Results with concurrent.futures

It's possible to retrieve and process outputs returned by jobs executed by ProcessPoolExecutor or ThreadPoolExecutor—instead of just printing them to stdout like you saw in process_pool_executor.py. Let's consider an example:

process_pool_executor_results.py
```
import concurrent.futures

def multiply(a, b):
    return a * b

if __name__ == "__main__":
    with concurrent.futures.ProcessPoolExecutor() as executor:
        futures = []
        for i in range(5):
            future = executor.submit(multiply, a=i, b=i)
            futures.append(future)

        for future in concurrent.futures.as_completed(futures):
            print(future.result())
```

If you run python3 process_pool_executor_results.py, you should see output roughly like the following:

```
0
16
1
4
9
```

This example is quite similar to the preceding example, but let's highlight a few key differences:

- Inside the with context manager, an empty list named futures is created.

- Every time we submit a job to the executor, the result of the submission is added to the futures list.

- The objects in the futures list represent the job submissions. We can use the objects to get results about jobs we have submitted.

- In particular, futures is passed to the concurrent.futures.as_completed function which yields the objects back after each underlying job has been completed.

- Calling .result() on the yielded objects gets the output of the job that was submitted.

- Ultimately, the output shows the results of the different multiplications we performed. Again, the order in this book may be distinct from the order of the output on your computer. The executor does not guarantee jobs will be completed in the order they were submitted.

Now let's see how concurrent.futures behaves when the underlying jobs raise exceptions.

Handling Exceptions

concurrent.futures can propagate exceptions from underlying jobs. Consider the following example:

process_pool_executor_exceptions.py

```
Line 1  import concurrent.futures

        def multiply(a, b):
            if a == 2:
    5           raise ValueError("Oops, a = 2")
            return a * b

        if __name__ == "__main__":
            with concurrent.futures.ProcessPoolExecutor() as executor:
    10          futures = []
                for i in range(5):
                    future = executor.submit(multiply, a=i, b=i)
                    futures.append(future)

    15          for future in concurrent.futures.as_completed(futures):
                    try:
                        print(future.result())
                    except ValueError:
                        print("Caught a ValueError")
```

If you run python3 process_pool_executor_exceptions.py, you should see output roughly like the following:

```
0
1
9
16
Caught a ValueError
```

The multiply function has been modified slightly in this example. Line 5 now raises a ValueError if the value of the a argument is 2. As before, the program submits five multiplication jobs to executor. The job results are processed as they complete. When future.result() is called on the job that submitted 2 for both a and b, the ValueError encountered in the multiply function is raised. The program prints out a message when it catches the ValueError.

Importantly, exceptions from the underlying jobs are raised and processed just like they would be in normal serially executed Python code. As long as you call future.result() it will either return the return value of your job, or it will raise the exception your job encountered and you can handle it.

Choosing ThreadPoolExecutor or ProcessPoolExecutor

Now that you've seen how to run code in threads or processes using Thread-PoolExecutor and ProcessPoolExecutor, which should you choose to use at any given time?

Let's revisit the table we saw earlier in this chapter:

Module	Paradigm	Object	Share Memory?	Restricted by GIL?
threading	threads	Thread	Yes	Yes
multiprocessing	processes	Process	No	No

The two primary differences between Thread and Process objects have to do with how memory is shared and how something called the GIL restricts performance.

First, we'll discuss memory sharing in Thread and Process objects.

Investigating Memory Sharing in Threads and Processes

In general, if you use the Thread object from the threading module, your "threaded" code will use the same memory space as its parent. Conversely, if you use the Process object from the multiprocessing object, your Python process will fork, and memory space will not be shared between the parent and child.

Let's illustrate the memory sharing dynamics with an example:

```
thread_memory.py
Line 1  import concurrent.futures

        a_list = []

 5
        def append_to_a_list():
            a_list.append(1)

        if __name__ == "__main__":
 10         with concurrent.futures.ThreadPoolExecutor() as executor:
                # note this is race condition prone code suitable only
                # for illustrative purposes
                executor.submit(append_to_a_list)
                executor.submit(append_to_a_list)
 15             executor.submit(append_to_a_list)

            print(a_list)
```

If you run the code python3 thread_memory.py, you should see the following output:

```
[1, 1, 1]
```

Line 3 defines a variable named a_list bound—initially—to an empty list []. Line 6 defines a function that appends 1 to the end of a_list. A ThreadPoolExecutor named executor is created, and three jobs are submitted to call the append_to_a_list function.

In the output, we see that a_list ultimately grew to three total entries: one added by the first executed job, a second added by the second executed job, and a third added by the third executed job: [1, 1, 1].

Avoid Sharing State

The preceding toy example shares state between multiple threads. Namely, the list a_list is manipulated by three separate jobs submitted to ThreadPoolExecutor. In general, it is not advisable to share objects between threads because many objects are not thread safe, and it may be possible to corrupt or introduce other unexpected problems if they are shared.[2] The example here is not generally recommended, but for illustrative purposes only.

In *Staying Safe When Writing Concurrent Code*, we will cover ways to structure concurrent programs that reduce the risk of corruption or other concurrency / thread safety issues.

---

2.   https://stackoverflow.com/a/6319267

As mentioned earlier, you now see how Thread objects can share memory with each other. In this example, Thread objects used their shared memory to append elements to the same list object.

Let's contrast the behavior of threads with an analogous example using Process objects:

process_memory.py
```
Line 1  import concurrent.futures

        a_list = []

  5

        def append_to_a_list():
            a_list.append(1)

        if __name__ == "__main__":
 10         with concurrent.futures.ProcessPoolExecutor() as executor:
                executor.submit(append_to_a_list)
                executor.submit(append_to_a_list)
                executor.submit(append_to_a_list)

 15         print(a_list)
```

If you run python3 process_memory.py, you should see the following output:

```
[]
```

The contents of process_memory.py are nearly identical to the contents of thread_memory.py. As before, a variable named a_list is—initially—bound to an empty list (line 3). A function named append_to_a_list is defined: it appends 1 to a_list (line 6). process_memory.py, however, instantiates Process objects instead of Thread objects (implicitly via ProcessPoolExecutor) to invoke the append_to_a_list function.

The end result is that a_list in the main program stays empty and the final output is [] (and not [1, 1, 1]). a_list in the main program never grows to three elements because each ProcessPoolExecutor job manipulates their own version of a_list and just adds one element to it and then exits. So, the final output remains the initial value of [] since each process has manipulated their own version of a_list.

Avoid Sharing State (Continued)

As with thread_memory.py, the process_memory.py example is for illustrative purposes only. While parts of these examples may not be strictly incorrect, they implement race condition–prone patterns that are not recommended for general use.

You can think of Process objects as creating a duplicate of the parent process and starting over. Thread objects, by contrast, continue to execute in generally the same context as their parent (including the ability to manipulate variables in the parent process).

Now that you've learned about memory-sharing differences between Thread and Process objects, let's move on to a second important difference: GIL restrictions.

Running Into GIL Restrictions for Threads and Processes

Revisiting our table from earlier...

Module	Paradigm	Object	Share Memory?	Restricted by GIL?
threading	threads	Thread	Yes	Yes
multiprocessing	processes	Process	No	No

What is the GIL and how exactly does it restrict Thread and Process objects? This is our next topic: let's start with an introduction to our new friend GIL.

Meet Our Friend GIL

Python programs are subject to a constraint known as the GIL: global interpreter lock. The GIL is part of Python's underlying implementation that restricts when and how the Python interpreter runs code.

Practically, what the GIL means is that—for a given Python process—only a single thread can be running Python operations at a given time. For example:

```
Thread A: executing.........executing.........
Thread B: .........executing.................
Thread C: ...........................executing
Has GIL : A--------B--------A--------C--------
```

In the example, only one of Thread A, B, or C are ever executing at a time. The thread currently executing is the one with the current global interpreter lock.

Practically, this means that using threads in a Python program won't necessarily speed up that program's execution. Let's demonstrate this reality with an example:

gil_example.py
```
import time

def do_work():
    countdown = 75000
    while countdown > 0:
        countdown -= 1
```

```
def run_comparision():
    start_serial = time.time()
    for _ in range(1000):
        do_work()
    elapsed_serial = time.time() - start_serial
    print(f"Serial execution took {elapsed_serial} seconds")

if __name__ == "__main__":
    run_comparision()
```

If you run python3 gil_example.py, your computer will execute it for a few seconds and you should see output like this:

```
Serial execution took 4.992825746536255 seconds
```

The code defines a function called do_work. do_work that subtracts 1 from 75000 successively until it reaches 0. The do_work function is executed 1000 times serially. Afterward, the program prints the number of seconds it took to execute the 1000 do_work calls. In my case, it took about five seconds. Your elapsed time will vary somewhat.

Expanding on the preceding example, we can run the same do_work function using threads:

gil_example_2.py
```
import concurrent.futures
import time

def do_work():
    countdown = 75000
    while countdown > 0:
        countdown -= 1

def run_comparision():
    start_serial = time.time()
    for _ in range(1000):
        do_work()
    elapsed_serial = time.time() - start_serial
    print(f"Serial execution took {elapsed_serial} seconds")

    start_threaded = time.time()
    with concurrent.futures.ThreadPoolExecutor() as executor:
        for _ in range(1000):
            executor.submit(do_work)
    elapsed_threaded = time.time() - start_threaded
    print(f"Threaded execution took {elapsed_threaded} seconds")

if __name__ == "__main__":
    run_comparision()
```

If you run python3 gil_example_2.py, your computer will again execute it for a few seconds and you should see output like this:

```
‹ Serial execution took 4.874225854873657 seconds
  Threaded execution took 4.986262083053589 seconds
```

This new code adds a few more lines that invoke the do_work function with threads via ThreadPoolExecutor.

Notably, the serial execution and threaded execution times are essentially the same (about five seconds each for me). Python threads haven't improved the performance of our program.

You've just demonstrated how the GIL (global interpreter lock) limits the ability of Python threads to improve the performance of programs that spend time running Python operations. Since only one thread could ever be doing work at a time, it wasn't really possible to improve the speed of this particular program using threads.

Why Is There a GIL at All?

The underlying implementation of Python itself deliberately includes the GIL. The GIL helps Python language contributors write Python itself in a memory safe way. Attempts have been made to remove the GIL from Python's underlying implementation, but as of this writing the GIL remains a part of Python.

Sidestepping the GIL with I/O

Importantly, if a thread is waiting for I/O like a web request or database access, it does *not* hold the GIL. So, it may be possible for Thread A to be waiting for the results of a web request while Thread B holds the GIL and is executing some Python code. The fact that the GIL doesn't impact waiting for I/O operations has important implications for our ability to speed up our code. Let's take a look at this in action:

speed_up.py
```
Line 1  import concurrent.futures
        import time
        from urllib import request

     5  def get_info():
            request.urlopen("https://example.com", timeout=30).read()

        def run_comparison():
            start_serial = time.time()
    10      for _ in range(25):
                get_info()
            elapsed_serial = time.time() - start_serial
            print(f"Serial execution took {elapsed_serial} seconds")
```

```
15      start_threaded = time.time()
        with concurrent.futures.ThreadPoolExecutor() as executor:
            for _ in range(25):
                executor.submit(get_info)
        elapsed_threaded = time.time() - start_threaded
20      print(f"Threaded execution took {elapsed_threaded} seconds")

    if __name__ == "__main__":
        run_comparison()
```

If you run python3 speed_up.py, you should receive output similar to the following:

```
Serial execution took 2.2511167526245117 seconds.
Threaded execution took 0.3836090564727783 seconds.
```

The preceding program defines a function named get_info on line 5. get_info uses the urllib.request standard library module to make a web request to example.com.[3] Lines 10 – 11 call the get_info function 25 times serially using a for loop. Lines 16 – 18 call the get_info function 25 times using threads via a ThreadPoolExecutor instance named executor.

The output on your computer will differ from my output, but generally the threaded execution time should be significantly faster. In my case, threaded took about 0.38 seconds where serial execution took about 2.25 seconds.

You've now seen how Python threads can help improve the speed of programs that are I/O bound.

GIL Affects Third-Party Packages Differently

 Note that some third-party libraries (for example, numpy) are able to perform math and other operations without being restrained by the GIL. This is true only on a case-by-case basis for third-party packages depending on their underlying implementations.

Writing with GIL Restrictions in Mind

Given what we know about the GIL, when should you use Thread objects, and when should you use Process objects? What is each good for, and when is it best to use them? The following table outlines general recommendations:

Module	Object	Helps CPU-Bound?	Helps I/O-Bound?
threading	Thread	No	Yes
multiprocessing	Process	Yes	Yes

---

3. https://example.com

In general, you should use Thread objects only if your program is I/O-bound. Process objects can be used for either CPU-bound or I/O-bound code.

Examples of I/O-bound operations include making a web request, reading a file, querying a database, and so on. Examples of CPU-bound operations include doing math and manipulating Python objects.

Creating a new Python Process has additional overhead that Python threads do not have, including pickling data in and out of the new processes. It's best to profile your program and your use case specifically to find out what combination of Threads and/or Processes suit your program best.

Writing concurrent code can be a tall order. As mentioned in the beginning of this chapter, it is easy to introduce bugs to your program when you add concurrency.

What can we do to help avoid unexpected bugs? We'll discuss this next.

Staying Safe When Writing Concurrent Code

In general, it is best to share as little as possible between different threads and processes. Problems tend to start as soon as you try to share objects between different thread or process objects.

Python does include a set of tools for locking and otherwise passing and sharing state when using Thread or Process objects including threading.Lock, threading.Barrier, threading.Semaphore, multiprocessing.Queue, and several others. The aforementioned tools are powerful and can be used to write elegant concurrent programs.

When writing the concurrent code, however, I find it helpful to follow a simple heuristic: share nothing. Even though Python provides powerful tools for writing concurrent programs, they are not the first thing I reach for—instead of using a tool like threading.Lock to coordinate threads, is it possible to create two threads that work without coordinating amongst themselves at all?

At its core, "share nothing" means avoiding writing code that looks similar to this:

```
share_nothing_wrong.py
def add_elements(a_list):
    a_list += ["a", "b", "c"]
    return a_list
```

```
if __name__ == "__main__":
    with ThreadPoolExecutor() as executor:
        # wrong: don't do the following
        shared_list = []
        executor.submit(add_elements, a_list=shared_list)
        executor.submit(add_elements, a_list=shared_list)
```

In this example, the list named shared_list is passed to multiple threads that each do something with it. Instead of sharing a list—which will eventually require careful locking and thought to appropriately guard access to that list—we can just share nothing and pass inputs and outputs directly:

share_nothing_right.py
```
from concurrent.futures import as_completed, ThreadPoolExecutor

def get_elements():
    return ["a", "b", "c"]

if __name__ == "__main__":
    with ThreadPoolExecutor() as executor:
        final_output = []
        future_1 = executor.submit(get_elements)
        future_2 = executor.submit(get_elements)

        for future in as_completed([future_1, future_2]):
            final_output += future.result()
        print(final_output)
```

This code is a slight modification of the "wrong" example. Instead of passing a list into Thread objects, we let the Thread objects construct new lists themselves and return them back to the parent process which combines them all before printing an output:

```
['a', 'b', 'c', 'a', 'b', 'c']
```

While both programs will generally return the same output, only the second example avoids sharing objects and thus eliminates many potential risks for introducing concurrency bugs.

If—and only if—you find the share nothing approach is unacceptably slow or cumbersome for your program, then consider using synchronization primitives like locks, semaphores, or queues. In my opinion, these synchronization primitives are not for the faint of heart and only should be used in very specific circumstances or on teams with high tolerance for errors. David Baron and Bobby Holley have a photo[4] that I think captures the spirt of this advice generally, as shown on page 83.

---

4.   https://bholley.net/blog/2015/must-be-this-tall-to-write-multi-threaded-code.html

Photo by David Baron and Bobby Holley.

The photo shows a programmer standing beneath a sign that says, "Must be this tall to write multi-threaded code." The sign is taped onto the wall several feet above the programmer's head. Effectively, the joke is that nobody is qualified to write multi-threaded code. While the photo is meant to be funny, I think it captures just how hard multi-threading and synchronization is to get right. My advice is to focus your time refining your program's abstractions and data flows before dabbling with multi-threading and synchronization.

If you're interested, you can learn more about these synchronization primitives in the Python standard library documentation online.[5]

Building with an Alternate Model: asyncio

A discussion of concurrency in Python is not complete without mentioning the asyncio module. asyncio is noteworthy for several reasons including that it is a recent addition to Python (arriving in Python 3.4) and includes its own special reserved keywords async and await.

So far, we've talked about using threads and processes in Python—neither of those had their own dedicated reserved keywords. asyncio is different than threads and processes primarily because asyncio relies on a programming paradigm called cooperative multitasking. The asyncio reserved keywords async and await help facilitate running code in this cooperative multitasking model.

---

5. https://docs.python.org/3/library/concurrency.html

What does cooperative multitasking mean? Let's learn more about cooperative multitasking in the following figure:

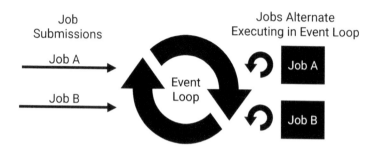

Effectively, a series of jobs are submitted to a single Python process running something called an event loop. The event loop is only ever executing a single job at a time. Each job, however, can explicitly surrender control back to the event loop when, for example, they are waiting for a web request to complete or performing some other long running operation, particularly one that is I/O bound. When a job surrenders control back to the event loop, another job gets to pick back up and start executing again.

In the preceding example, Job A and Job B each share time executing in the event loop. When Job A surrenders control back to the event loop, Job B can start executing. When Job B surrenders control back to the event loop, Job A can continue executing. This dance continues until the jobs have completed.

The async keyword allows functions to mark themselves as being able to surrender control back to the event loop. The await keyword allows specific lines to actually surrender control back to the event loop.

Event loop programming and asyncio can be considered an alternative line of thinking and frame of reference to run Python code under. Not all standard library modules are fully compliant with asyncio principles. For example time.sleep() does not surrender back time to the event loop and so a special variant asyncio.sleep() has to be called to surrender back to the event loop. The Python built-in open function for manipulating files, similarly, doesn't surrender back time to the asyncio event loop while waiting for I/O. So—if you choose to use asyncio—you have to consciously select special asyncio-compatible functions and third-party libraries to take full advantage of event-loop programming.

Consider, for example, if we wrote a hello world program using asyncio:

```
asyncio_hello_world.py
import asyncio

async def sleep_then_say_hello():
    await asyncio.sleep(1)
    print("hello")

async def sleep_then_say_world():
    await asyncio.sleep(1)
    print("world")

async def main():
    # simultaneously spawn both sleep_then_say_hello and
    # sleep_then_say_world
    await asyncio.gather(sleep_then_say_hello(), sleep_then_say_world())

asyncio.run(main())
```

There's a lot of syntax in this file, but the net of it is that you define async functions that you can later await on. In this case, we await on two functions—one that prints hello and another that prints world. Notably, to implement the sleeps, it was important that we used asyncio.sleep so that our program could yield back time to the event loop. asyncio.gather submits both jobs to the event loop to print both hello and world. You can try running this Python program just like you'd run any other Python program: python3 asyncio_hello_word.py.

Should you use asyncio instead of threads and processes? The answer is complicated.

Running many tasks in a single asyncio event loop has a lower overhead than spawning the equivalent number of threads or processes using Thread and Process objects. Does that mean your code will be faster? Not necessarily. Your code may not surrender control back to the event loop when it can or should—for example, if you don't use appropriate third-party libraries or asyncio compatible standard library modules. It's also possible to overwhelm an event loop with too many tasks, so that some tasks never appear to start or complete because they are constantly waiting for their turn to be executed. asyncio code is also still subject same concurrency pitfalls like race conditions and deadlocks outlined in forewarning at the beginning of this chapter. asyncio is not a silver bullet (and threads and processes aren't either).

In general, my recommendation is to use concurrency in specific and isolated ways. If concurrency pervades your program—with threads and processes or asyncio concepts strewn everywhere—your code will be hard to reason about.

If your code is hard to reason about, it will have more bugs. Try to keep it simple and remember: share nothing.

There's a lot to learn about asyncio, but it won't be covered in this book. If you're interested in learning more, I recommend starting with the official asyncio documentation.[6]

Wrapping Up

In this chapter, you learned about threads and processes, the concurrent.futures module, the global interpreter lock, and even touched on the relatively new asyncio module. You now have a good working mental model of how concurrency works in Python should you choose that your code needs concurrency.

Now that we have a good understanding of Python's fundamentals, we can look at common traps Python programs get caught in and how to avoid them.

---

6.   https://docs.python.org/3/library/asyncio.html

## CHAPTER 4

Avoiding Traps

Many of my favorite foods are junk foods: ice cream, Oreos with milk, Nutter Butters, chocolate chip cookies, and the like. If my pantry has any of these foods in it, I will eat them—enjoying a glass of milk and Oreos is a simple pleasure that I've indulged in more than my fair share of times.

Being gluttonous is fun sometimes, but staying in shape and healthy are also important to me. One time I ate a whole bag of Oreos and couldn't stomach much else for the next few days. So, I have to strike a balance to avoid trapping myself in a situation where I might eat too many Oreos. Since I know that I'll eat any delicious junk food that gets into my house, I have to stop the problem at the source. I can't ever buy any junk food, because then I know I am guaranteed to eat it.

In a similar way, Python has its own share of junk food. Delicious parts of the standard library that, if used too much, can trap your Python project in an unhealthy situation. To keep a Python project in check, we must be diligent to avoid falling into traps that might hurt us.

You've already encountered and used important parts of standard library including—most recently—tools for concurrency. In this chapter, though, you will focus on the dangers of the pickle module, datetime objects without time-zones, and mutable default function arguments. After reading this chapter, you will have some additional knowledge to help you make healthy decisions in your Python project.

Serializing Python Objects with the pickle Module

Python only includes one standard library module named after a food, and that module is named pickle. The pickle module allows arbitrary Python objects to be serialized into a stream of bytes. This stream of bytes can then be unpickled by another Python program to restore the object that was originally pickled. Let's explore this in a little more detail.

In the following example pickle is used to serialize and de-serialize a list containing strings and None:

pickle_example.py
```
import pickle

l = ["a", "b", None, "c"]

dumped_l = pickle.dumps(l)
print(dumped_l)

loaded_l = pickle.loads(dumped_l)
print(loaded_l)
```

If you run python3 pickle_example.py, you should see output like the following:

```
b'\x80\x03]q\x00(X\x01\x00\x00\x00aq\x01X\x01\x00\x00\x00bq\x02NX\x01\x00
\x00\x00cq\x03e.'
['a', 'b', None, 'c']
```

import pickle makes the pickle module available to our program. A list with strings and None is assigned to the variable l. pickle.dumps(l) returns bytes which are assigned to the dumped_l variable and printed out: this is the pickled representation of the l list. Calling pickle.loads(dumped_l) unpickles the bytes back into a Python object—in this case, a list identical to l which we started with.

The pickle Module Is Not Secure

 Never unpickle data from untrusted sources. The process of unpickling data can execute arbitrary code on your computer, allowing malicious actors to steal, alter, or otherwise compromise your machine.

---

pickle can allow you to—effectively—save out a Python object so you can reload it to use it later.

pickle works with more than just primitive types. You can also use pickle to dump and load a custom class you have written. Behind the scenes, Python also uses pickle internally to, for example, transport objects between different Python processes when you use the multiprocessing module.

As noted in the preceding warning box, however, pickle is not secure. If you load an untrusted pickle file, you are effectively giving a third party the ability to execute arbitrary code on your computer. So, among the other problems pickle introduces (problems we'll explore next), loading pickled data is a massive security vulnerability to have lurking in your application.

Running Into Trouble Over Time with pickle

Beyond its security issues, pickle does not fare well when code changes over time. Consider the following example:

pickle_over_time.py
```
import pickle

class Snack:
    def __init__(self):
        self.cookie = "Oreo"

snack_dumped = pickle.dumps(Snack())

class Snack:
    def __init__(self):
        self.cookie = "Oreo"
        self.drink = "milk"

snack_loaded = pickle.loads(snack_dumped)
print(snack_loaded.drink)
```

If you run python3 pickle_over_time.py, you should see output like the following:

```
Traceback (most recent call last):
  File "pickle_over_time.py", line 15, in <module>
    print(snack_loaded.drink)
AttributeError: 'Snack' object has no attribute 'drink'
```

First, a class named Snack is defined. The Snack class has a single attribute cookie that is initially bound to a value of "Oreo". An instance of Snack is pickled by calling pickle.dumps. Then, a new version of the Snack class is defined. The new version of the Snack class includes an additional instance variable: drink. The instance variable drink is initially bound to a value of "milk". The earlier Snack instance is then loaded by calling pickle.loads. Trying to access drink on that unpickled Snack instantly results in an AttributeError Exception.

The AttributeError Exception is raised because the pickle'd bytes we loaded, were sourced from a version of the Snack class that did not have the drink attribute. Somewhat confusingly, the object was still successfully unpickled and placed inside an instance of the new definition of the Snack class.

Admittedly, this example may feel a little contrived because the classes are simple and there aren't too many lines of code. The point it illustrates, however, is that unpickling an old pickle file may not work as seamlessly as you might expect. If some amount of time has passed and code has changed, you could inadvertently pickle out old objects that are no longer compatible with your application but still masquerade as valid objects. In the preceding example, the loaded Snack instance seems correct because it is an instance of the same Snack class. Unfortunately, the program then starts to fail when a new attribute is accessed.

It can be tempting to think, "I know the bounds of my applications and we'll never load this pickle file from somewhere I don't trust or at a time we didn't expect." As time passes, though, your project may have evolved as you added new features or started collaborating with others. After this time, it suddenly may be possible for someone to hijack your system by feeding it malicious pickle files in a way you hadn't initially expected. At the very least—even with careful design—a small, internal refactoring of a class like adding self.drink = "milk" can break existing pickle files.

Many projects wind up living and dying on copy paste. If a pickle usage exists once in the code base, there's a good chance someone else will copy paste the pattern and use it for some other purpose. Before you know it, your pickle usage has proliferated and some of those new usages may be insecure or bug-ridden.

Now that we have seen some of the risks associated with using the pickle module, let's explore some alternatives.

Choosing Alternatives to pickle

pickle may beckon with its ability to serialize and de-serialize virtually any Python object, but its security and object integrity issues make it a dangerous pattern to embrace generally. My recommendation is to strongly reconsider pickle usages in your projects.

Frequently, serialization and de-serialization libraries like pickle appear near application edges. For example, an application might read data from a file, process and enrich that data and then pass on that enriched data to another application. The transfer point where the enriched data is passed to another application might be considered an application edge: one application is ending and transferring data and another is beginning and receiving data. How should this data be transferred? What format can both processes read? How convenient is it for each application to serialize and de-serialize that data?

There is no lack of alternative serialization and de-serialization packages other than pickle. To name a few:

- JSON
- Protocol Buffers
- Apache Parquet

JSON is a ubiquitous serialization and deserialization format natively supported by the Python standard library via the json module.[1] Google offers its Protocol Buffers package for compact and efficient object serialization and deserialization.[2] Apache Parquet offers a columnar data format especially well suited to applications that store large amounts of row-based data.[3] SQLite databases (as you learned about on page 55) can even be used as a serialization format to pass or otherwise share structured data between processes.

pickle is often times more convenient than any of the alternatives listed. Since you might have a Python object already, it makes sense to want to capture that Python object exactly using pickle. It's true that serializing to JSON, Protocol Buffers, and so on, may require more work and writing additional translation code. These alternative formats, however, are more secure. Further, these formats are language independent, which make them less liable to bite you later when your Python objects change and old pickle data can no longer dutifully construct the objects you are interested in.

The pickle module may beckon to you. "Ah, if I just used pickle, I could solve this caching problem I'm having right now and be on with my day." I urge you to resist the siren call of the pickle module. If you need to serialize data, write it out as JSON, parquet, or some other standard format without code injection vulnerabilities: focus on transporting your data more than trying to transport your classes.

Beyond traps related to object serialization and deserialization, keeping track of time in your programs contains its own set of traps. We'll explore these next.

Handling Datetimes with Timezones

Python's datetime module allows your programs to manipulate dates and times in high-level ways. You can, for example, use arithmetic to calculate the difference between dates and advance dates forward and backward through time.

This section introduces a particularly thorny part of the datetime library: dealing with timezones. You won't need to know the ins and outs of the datetime module to follow along with this section, but feel free to consult the Python datetime docs if you are interested.[4]

---

1. https://docs.python.org/3/library/json.html
2. https://developers.google.com/protocol-buffers/
3. http://parquet.apache.org
4. https://docs.python.org/3/library/datetime.html

Using datetime with and without Timezones

Python provides the datetime object to represent specific points in time (for example, October 11th 2020 at 7:42 p.m.). By design, Python allows users to work with two variants of datetime objects: datetimes with timezones, and datetimes without timezones.

Here is an example of datetime object with a timezone:

```
>>> from datetime import datetime, timezone
>>> datetime.now(timezone.utc)
datetime.datetime(2020, 10, 11, 19, 42, 43, 976988, tzinfo=datet
ime.timezone.utc)
```

Calling datetime.now(timezone.utc) returns a datetime object representing the current time in the UTC timezone. This is a datetime with a timezone. The tzinfo attribute of the datetime is filled in with the timezone.utc object passed into the now function.

What Is UTC?

UTC (coordinated universal time) is a timezone that is never adjusted for daylight savings. Other timezones often describe themselves in terms of offset from UTC. For example, a timezone might be 7 hours behind UTC or 7 hours ahead of UTC. Since UTC only ever moves forward in time (as opposed to timezones that dial their clocks forwards and backwards for daylight savings), datetimes in UTC are useful as references.

Here are two examples of creating datetime objects without timezones:

```
>>> from datetime import datetime
>>> datetime.now()
datetime.datetime(2020, 10, 11, 12, 42, 46, 953011)
>>> print(datetime.now().tzinfo)
None
>>> print(datetime.utcnow().tzinfo)  # utcnow() also omits tzinfo
None
```

In contrast with the first example, calling datetime.now() with no arguments returns a datetime object without any timezone information (its tzinfo atrribute is set to None). Although there is no timezone information associated with this datetime, datetime.now() returns a local time (in other words, a time consistent with the timezone your operating system is currently set to). For example, if your computer is set up in Los Angeles, California, datetime.now() will return the current wall clock time in Los Angeles.

The last call in the previous example shows that the utcnow function provided by the datetime module also returns a datetime without a timezone.[5] The datetime returned by utcnow is the current UTC wall clock time, but—like the call to now with no arguments—no tzinfo object is attached.

datetime objects with timezones are often referred to as "timezone aware" datetime objects. datetime objects without timezones are often referred to as, "timezone naive" datetime objects. We'll explore some of the problems at the intersection of timezone naive and timezone aware datetime objects in the next section.

Trying to Mix Timezone Aware and Timezone Naive datetimes

Now that we have a sense of the difference between timezone aware and timezone naive datetime objects, let's see what happens when we try to mix the two:

```
>>> from datetime import datetime, timezone
>>> utc_now = datetime.now(timezone.utc)
>>> local_now = datetime.now()
>>> is_greater = local_now > utc_now
Traceback (most recent call last):
  File "<stdin>", line 1, in <module>
TypeError: can't compare offset-naive and offset-aware datetimes
```

In this example, a timezone aware datetime is built and bound to the variable named utc_now. Next, a timezone naive datetime is constructed and bound to the variable named local_now. When local_now and utc_now are compared using the greater-than operator, Python raises an exception and complains that it cannot compare naive and aware datetime objects.

Indeed, Python prohibits from meaningfully mixing timezone naive and timezone aware datetime objects even with operators other than greater than:

```
>>> utc_now - utc_now
datetime.timedelta(0)
>>> local_now - local_now
datetime.timedelta(0)
>>> local_now - utc_now
Traceback (most recent call last):
  File "<stdin>", line 1, in <module>
TypeError: can't subtract offset-naive and offset-aware datetimes
```

The preceding example demonstrates that it's possible to subtract timezone aware datetime objects from each other, or timezone naive datetime objects from each other. Subtracting utc_now or local_now from themselves, for example, yields

---

5. https://docs.python.org/3/library/datetime.html#datetime.datetime.utcnow

a timedelta difference of 0. However, a TypeError is raised when local_now - utc_now is executed because Python forbids mixing naive and aware datetime objects.

We've now learned about the two primary variants of datetime objects available to Python programs: timezone aware and timezone naive. We've also seen that Python generally forbids mixing timezone aware and timezone naive datetime objects. Before we introduce a set of utilities that will allow us to work effectively with both timezone aware and timezone naive datetime objects, we'll explore how timezone naive datetime objects may introduce additional ambiguity into your programs.

Understanding Ambiguity Introduced by Timezone Naive datetimes

One of the trickiest parts about representing datetimes involves region-specific handling of daylight savings. Different parts of the world have different rules for daylight savings—periods of time when clocks are "reset" to a different time to, for example, make sunset occur later or earlier in the evening.

Consider what happens in California in November 2020 when daylight savings ends:

1.   November 1, 2020 1 a.m.–2 a.m. occurs.
2.   Clocks are reset back an hour to 1 a.m.
3.   November 1, 2020 1 a.m.–2 a.m. occurs *AGAIN*.

Confusingly—especially for software systems—all the points in time between 1 a.m. and 2 a.m. on November 1, 2020 occur twice. For example, 1:35 a.m. on November 1, 2020 occurs once before the clocks are reset and a second time after the clocks are reset.

Let's pretend a program running on a server in California is directed to do something on November 1, 2020 at 1:35 a.m. Does that mean it should do something the first time 1:35 a.m. occurs, the second time 1:35 a.m. occurs, or both times 1:35 a.m. occurs? What if the program isn't running in a place, like California, where daylight savings ends at this time? Should the program behave differently when it's run in different regions?

Answers to these questions tend to depend on the specific application being run, but it is easy to forget about these situations as an application is developed.

We've now seen that Python refuses to mix timezone naive and timezone aware datetime objects, and that timezone naive datetime objects bring along their own implicit ambiguity. In the next section we'll resolve some of this conflict and see how to work effectively with datetime objects.

Writing Functions for Handling Timezones

In order to work with datetime objects in Python, we want to reduce the number of unexpected, "can't compare offset-naive and offset-aware datetimes" exceptions we see and also reduce the amount of implicit ambiguity of datetime objects themselves by avoiding daylight savings.

To help accomplish these goals, we can use following three timezone util functions:

```
timezone_utils.py
# alternatively: `from backports.zoneinfo import ZoneInfo` if you
# are on Python <= 3.9 and have installed backports.zoneinfo
from zoneinfo import ZoneInfo

def is_aware(dt_value):
    """Returns True if dt_value is timezone aware. False otherwise"""
    return (
        dt_value.tzinfo is not None
        and dt_value.tzinfo.utcoffset(dt_value) is not None
    )

def make_aware(dt_value, timezone_name):
    """Make dt_value an aware datetime in the given timezone_name"""
    if is_aware(dt_value):
        raise ValueError("dt_value is already aware")
    zone_info = ZoneInfo(timezone_name)
    return dt_value.replace(tzinfo=zone_info)

def change_timezone(dt_value, timezone_name):
    """
    Change the timezone associated to dt_value to the given timezone_name
    """
    if not is_aware(dt_value):
        raise ValueError("Must pass a timezone aware dt_value")
    zone_info = ZoneInfo(timezone_name)
    return dt_value.astimezone(zone_info)
```

These functions allow you to do the following:

1. Determine if a given datetime object is timezone aware or not using is_aware.

2. Make a timezone naive datetime object into a timezone aware one using make_aware.

3. Transition a timezone aware datetime object into a different timezone using change_timezone.

zoneinfo Module Availability

The zoneinfo module was introduced in Python 3.9 (released in October 2020).[6] To use the functions in timezone_utils.py, you will need Python 3.9 or to have the zoneinfo backport installed to make the zoneinfo module available.[7] If you are using this book's companion Docker image, you are ready to go. Otherwise you can see an example of the backports installation on page 107. Windows systems will also need the first-party tzdata pip package (to account for Windows lack of a built-in IANA timezone database).[8]

Let's consider some examples using the three functions from timezone_utils.py. If you load the code in timezone_utils.py into your Python interactive console, you can follow along.

```
>>> from datetime import datetime
>>> nov_1st_135_am = datetime(2020, 11, 1, 1, 35)
>>> is_aware(nov_1st_135_am)
False
```

In this first example, a timezone naive datetime object is constructed that represents November 1, 2020 at 1:35 a.m. and is bound to the variable named nov_1st_135_am. Calling is_aware on nov_1st_135_am returns False confirming that the datetime object is not timezone aware.

Now that we've confirmed we have a timezone naive datetime, let's make it aware:

```
>>> nov_1st_135_am = datetime(2020, 11, 1, 1, 35)
>>> make_aware(nov_1st_135_am, timezone_name="America/Los_Angeles")
datetime.datetime(2020, 11, 1, 1, 35, tzinfo=zoneinfo.ZoneInfo(key=
'America/Los_Angeles'))
```

Continuing with the November 1st 1:35AM datetime object, we make the datetime object timezone aware by calling make_aware with the America/Los_Angeles timezone. make_aware returns a new datetime object that is timezone aware and in the America/Los_Angeles datetime.

As we mentioned in an earlier section, November 1, 2020 at 1:35 a.m. is a significant time in California because it occurs twice:

1. November 1, 2020 1 a.m.–2 a.m. occurs.
2. Clocks are reset back an hour to 1 a.m.
3. November 1, 2020 1 a.m.–2 a.m. occurs *AGAIN*.

---

6. https://docs.python.org/3.9/whatsnew/3.9.html
7. https://pypi.org/project/backports.zoneinfo/
8. https://pypi.org/project/tzdata/

datetime Objects Are Immutable

 datetime objects in Python are immutable. This means that it is not possible to change a datetime object instance in any way. For example, you cannot actually change the tzinfo attribute on any datetime object. What you can do, however, is call a function that returns a new datetime object identical to the first one but with tzinfo (or some other attribute) replaced with a new value. When we, for example, call the make_aware function with some input datetime object, that input object itself is not changed. An entirely new object is constructed and returned instead.

So, when we called make_aware(nov_1st_135_am, timezone_name="America/Los_Angeles"), does the returned value represent a time during period 1 (the first occurrence of 1 a.m.–2 a.m.), or does the returned value represent a time during period 2 (the second occurrence of 1 a.m.–2 a.m.)?

We'll use the fold attribute of the datetime object and the change_timezone function to determine exactly what time we are representing:

```
>>> nov_1st_135_am = datetime(2020, 11, 1, 1, 35)
>>> aware = make_aware(nov_1st_135_am, timezone_name="America/Los_Angeles")
>>> print(aware.fold)
0
>>> change_timezone(aware, "UTC")
datetime.datetime(2020, 11, 1, 8, 35, tzinfo=zoneinfo.ZoneInfo(key='UTC'))
```

datetime objects include an attribute named fold. fold must be either 0 or 1 (and defaults to 0). When fold is 0, the datetime represents the beginning of a transition (that is, the first occurrence of 1:35 a.m. in our November 1, 2020 in California example). When fold is 1, the datetime represents the end of the transition (that is, the second occurrence of 1:35 a.m. in our November 1, 2020 in California example). Let's see the difference when we use fold=1 on the same datetime:

```
>>> nov_1st_135_am = datetime(2020, 11, 1, 1, 35)
>>> aware = make_aware(nov_1st_135_am, timezone_name="America/Los_Angeles")
>>> aware = aware.replace(fold=1)
>>> print(aware.fold)
1
>>> change_timezone(aware, timezone_name="UTC")
datetime.datetime(2020, 11, 1, 9, 35, tzinfo=zoneinfo.ZoneInfo(key='UTC'))
```

When fold is 1, the datetime object named aware represents the second occurrence of 1:35 a.m. The first/second distinction is clear when we change the timezone of aware to "UTC". When fold is 0, the UTC datetime is for 8 a.m., and when fold is 1, the UTC datetime is for 9 a.m. (a one-hour difference).

Now that you're armed with the is_aware, make_aware, and change_timezone functions from the previous section, you are well equipped to successfully handle datetime objects in your Python program.

Summarizing datetime Recommendations

Many successful Python projects follow these three directives to use Python datetime objects effectively:

1. Always use timezone aware datetime objects in the UTC timezone internally in your program.

2. Never use timezone naive datetimes in your program.

3. Only change from UTC to another timezone when you need to display a time to a user.

To ensure you always use timezone aware UTC datetime objects, you can

- Get the current time by saying: datetime.now(timezone.utc)
- Immediately convert user submitted times to UTC using make_aware and/or change_timezone

In the final section of this chapter, we will investigate and rectify traps that can appear inside of Python function signatures.

Getting Caught with Sticky Default Arguments

Python allows you to specify arguments with defaults in your function signatures. For example, consider the use_exclamation argument in the print_greeting function:

```
def print_greeting(name, use_exclamation=False):
    greeting = "Hello " + name
    if use_exclamation:
        greeting += "!"
    print(greeting)
```

In the above example, the use_exclamation argument to the print_greeting function has a default value of False. Since use_exclamation defaults to False, print_greeting("David") outputs Hello David (with no trailing ! character). If we provided a value for the use_exclamation argument, however, the output changes. print_greeting("David", use_exclamation=True) outputs Hello David! because the value for use_exclamation is now True instead of its default value of False.

Default arguments are quite useful, and you'll see them appear in almost any Python code you encounter. In the standard library, for example, the sorted built-in function includes a reverse argument that defaults to False. The reverse argument allows the following useful modulation:

- sorted([3, 1, 2]) returns [1, 2, 3]
- sorted([3, 1, 2], reverse=True) returns [3, 2, 1]

Default arguments have one gotcha that has bitten many Python programmers. We'll discuss this gotcha next.

Binding Early: Problems with Default Arguments

Despite the prevalence and usefulness of default arguments, they can sometimes cause unexpected problems. Consider the following dangerous example that defines a function named add_to_list:

mutable_default_argument_wrong.py
```
# wrong:
def add_to_list(a_list=[]):
    a_list.append(2)
    print(a_list)

add_to_list()
add_to_list()
add_to_list()
add_to_list()
```

If you run the code, you should see output like the following:

```
[2]
[2, 2]
[2, 2, 2]
[2, 2, 2, 2]
```

Upon first inspection, it seems like add_to_list should create a new list every time it is called. The default argument a_list=[] seems to imply that if a_list is not explicitly provided, it should be bound to a new empty list. As seen in the sample output, however, this is not the case. It turns out, that the same exact list object is bound to a_list for every single call to add_to_list that doesn't explicitly provide a value for a_list. The end result is that the four add_to_list calls each append 2 to the same exact list.

The behavior shown previously is not a bug. Python evaluates default arguments once (when the function is loaded by the interpreter). So, if a mutable value is present as the default argument (for example, a list or a dictionary), that same object is used for every single function call. For immutable objects (like strings, datetime, integers, booleans, and None), it's fine to use the same exact object instance every time (since the object itself can't be changed).

The previous example isn't wrong, but it is dangerous because developers may expect the function to behave differently than it does. Developers passively reading def add_to_list(a_list=[]) might presume add_to_list will create a new list if no value is provided for a_list. Indeed, that's what the function looks like it should do.

Whenever I audit a Python code base, one of the first things I scan for are mutable default arguments. In the next section we'll discuss the correct pattern for when you want to use mutable default arguments.

Write Mutable Default Arguments Safely

To avoid the problems demonstrated in mutable_default_argument_wrong.py, you can use None as a sentinel value for a_list in the argument signature:

```
mutable_default_argument_right.py
# right:
def add_to_list(a_list=None):
    if a_list is None:
        a_list = []
    a_list.append(2)
    print(a_list)

add_to_list()
add_to_list()
add_to_list()
add_to_list()
```

If you run the code, you should see output like the following:

```
[2]
[2]
[2]
[2]
```

The previous dangerous example has been modified slightly. Instead of binding a_list to [] as its default the function signature, a_list is now bound to the sentinel value of None. If no value is provided for a_list in the function call, the function body creates a new empty list and assigns it to a_list. At the end of the day, this means that each of the four calls to add_to_list uses a brand new list object. Each call prints out [2], because no list objects are ever shared between function calls.

In general, when dealing with default arguments, the recommended pattern is to use None as a sentinel value / stand in for the empty data structure as shown earlier.

Detecting Mutable Default Arguments with flake8-bugbear

As we mentioned in Running Additional Checks with flake8-bugbear, on page 23, if you install the static analysis tool flake8 and its companion flake8-bugbear, you can automatically detect and forbid the use of mutable default arguments.[a,b] This helps prevent you and your teammates from falling—even accidentally—into the mutable default argument trap.

For example, the file mutable_default_argument_wrong.py (see code on page 99) has the the mutable default argument trap of def add_to_list(a_list=[]). After installing flake8 and flake8-bugbear (something already done for you if you are using this book's companion Docker image[c]) you can detect the trap using a command like this:

flake8 --show-source mutable_default_argument_wrong.py

If you run this, you should see an output line—among several others—that includes the following error about using mutable defaults:

```
❮ mutable_default_argument_wrong.py:2:24: B006 Do not use mutable data
  structures for argument defaults.  They are created during function
  definition time. All calls to the function reuse this one instance
  of that data structure, persisting changes between them.
  def add_to_list(a_list=[]):
                         ^
```

flake8 + flake8-bugbear dutifully reports that binding I to [] is liable to cause problems and should be removed. A nice automatic quality control to have in place!

---

a.   https://pypi.org/project/flake8/
b.   https://pypi.org/project/flake8-bugbear/
c.   https://github.com/DavidMuller/intuitive-python-book

Wrapping Up

In this chapter you've learned about some common traps to avoid in Python. In particular, you are primed to favor json (and other alternative libraries) over pickle, to always use timezone aware datetime objects in UTC, and to carefully avoid using mutable values like lists as defaults in your function signatures.

Next, we'll explore how to shepherd your Python projects into green fields even as you face external challenges and unexpected problems. Among other topics, you'll learn how to securely install third-party packages and keep your variables from being unexpectedly clobbered or shadowed.

## CHAPTER 5

Standing Guard When Python Breaks Free

You've heard of *Jurassic Park*, right? In case you haven't, the plot goes like this: a group of people showcase genetically modified dinosaurs in a purpose-built amusement park on a remote island. The dinosaurs are bred in a laboratory and engineered to require a specific chemical that can only be produced by the laboratory. Ostensibly, the dinosaurs are under control because they rely on the laboratory to provide this essential chemical.

Sure enough and without too much trouble, the dinosaurs find a way to obtain the chemical on their own. They start to cause problems at the park. Several movies and many wonderfully entertaining T-Rex chase scenes ensue.

Jurassic Park might be an entertaining book and movie, but how does that help us write better Python?

Almost every code base I've worked on is a little like Jurassic Park. An island full of people and monsters. A living, breathing, ecosphere of life that is often inches from going off the rails.

Maybe the codebase you work on feels a bit more tame; it may feel like everything is actually under control. That sense of security can feel good and be well-founded at times. There is a lot to be learned, however, about how to live peacefully with the dinosaurs that are lurking in the mist.

We want our code to be resilient to failure and resistant to tampering from malicious actors, and we want teammates who feel confident and comfortable with the system we are building.

Evolving from our work in the last chapter on avoiding common traps and pitfalls in Python, you will now learn techniques for hardening and harnessing your code so it provides maximal utility to you and your team. We will discuss securing third-party package installation, privatization in Python, keeping your tests organized, and the risks of variable shadowing.

Installing Third-Party Packages Securely with pip

Python's built-in third-party package manager is called pip. pip allows you to download third-party Python packages from the internet and use them in your programs. In this section you'll learn how to mitigate some of the dangers inherent to pip as you use it to download packages.

Running pip

You can try running pip by executing the following:

```
python3 -m pip --version
```

If you run this command, you should see output roughly like the following:

```
pip 20.2.3 from /home/monty/code/my-virtual-env/lib/python3.9/site-packa
ges/pip (python 3.9)
```

Your output may be slightly different if, for example, you are using a different version of Python, pip, or have Python installed in a different location. That's OK—our goal here is just to verify that you can run pip.

The -m Flag

The -m flag in the python3 -m pip --version command instructs Python to run the pip module (emphasis on "m"). While you can omit the leading python3 -m and just say pip --version to invoke pip, the python3 -m invocation style makes it clear exactly which python executable you want to run pip with. This can be useful if your system has multiple python executables (for example, if you use the venv module) and you want to ensure you install packages so they are available to the appropriate python executable.

It's important to install third-party Python packages on your computer in an isolated fashion. Since some operating systems use Python for their own purposes, it's good to install third-party packages in a separate place so as not to accidentally corrupt your operating system's Python installation.

Installing packages in an isolated way may also be important if you have two projects that implement two different applications—let's say one is a calculator and one is a printer. The calculator and printer might both use third-party Python packages. Importantly, they may even require different versions of the same package: the calculator might need version 1 of package X, but the printer might need version 8 of package X.

Before we move on with actually running any pip commands, we'll go over how to run pip in an isolated way on your system using virtual environments.

Creating Virtual Environments

As you might already know, Python provides a built-in mechanism for installing packages in isolated locations on your computer: the venv module in the standard library.

The venv module allows you to create so-called "virtual environments." Virtual environments are standalone directories that contain an isolated set of Python binaries and third-party packages installed by pip. You can have multiple virtual environments—one virtual environment for each of your projects, for example.

To create a virtual environment, run the following command:

```
python3 -m venv my-virtual-env
```

This will create a virtual environment in the current directory named my-virtual-env. It can be important to explicitly specify python3 because some operating systems still, by default, bind python to a Python 2 interpreter. We want to ensure, however, that our new virtual environment is set up for Python 3.

Virtual environments are really just directories with files. The my-virtual-environment directory created in the preceding command, for example, will contain a bin subdirectory with fresh Python executables:

```
$ python3 -m venv my-virtual-env
$ ls my-virtual-env/bin
Activate.ps1  activate.csh   easy_install      pip   pip3.9  python3
activate      activate.fish  easy_install-3.9  pip3  python  python3.9
```

When we list the files in the bin/ subdirectory of the virtual environment, you see binaries for both python and pip. Since virtual environments are just directories, if you are unhappy with a virtual environment, you can always just delete its directory and create a new one.

Slight Differences in Windows

 If you are on a Windows systems, the location of the virtual environment executables will be slightly different. They might appear in a C:\> my-virtual-env\Scripts\ directory, for example, instead of bin/.

Next let's try calling one of the newly installed binaries in the bin/ subdirectory of the virtual environment:

```
$ my-virtual-env/bin/python
Python 3.9.2 (default, Mar 12 2021, 18:54:15)
[GCC 8.3.0] on linux
Type "help", "copyright", "credits" or "license" for more information.
>>>
```

Calling my-virtual-env/bin/python, for example, launches the virtual environment's Python interpreter.

You may have noticed a few extra files in the my-virtual-env/bin/ subdirectory containing the word activate. These activate helper scripts can update the shell of your choice to point at the virtual environment Python binaries by default. For example, if you use the bash or zsh shells, you can run source my-virtual-env/bin/activate.

Before running source my-virtual-env/bin/activate, my shell behaves this way when I try to invoke python:

```
$ which python
/usr/local/bin/python
```

Calling which python indicates that python currently points to my system's default Python installation.

After running source my-virtual-env/bin/activate, however, my shell behaves like this:

```
$ source my-virtual-env/bin/activate
(my-virtual-env) $ which python
/home/monty/code/my-virtual-env/bin/python
```

Now, which python indicates that python points to the virtual environment Python we created earlier. The activate script also updated my shell's prompt so that it begins with a parenthetical calling out the name of the currently activated virtual environment (my-virtual-env). Calling the activate scripts isn't strictly necessary, but it can be convenient because you won't need to type out full paths to the virtual environment binaries. Different shells have different activate scripts: activate supports bash and zsh, activate.fish supports the fish shell and so on.

After running an activate script, you can run deactivate to remove the shims added to your shell that made the virtual environment binaries your defaults:

```
$ source my-virtual-env/bin/activate
(my-virtual-env) $ which python
/home/monty/code/my-virtual-env/bin/python
(my-virtual-env) $ deactivate
$ which python
/usr/local/bin/python
```

After running deactivate, python stopped pointing to the virtual environment Python binary. The prompt Python inserted at the beginning of my shell was removed, and python now points to /usr/local/bin/python.

For the remainder of this section, you should use a virtual environment anytime you run a pip command. You can call the virtual environment pip directly using its full path:

```
$ my-virtual-env/bin/python -m pip --version
pip 20.2.3 from /home/monty/code/my-virtual-env/lib/python3.9/site-packa
ges/pip (python 3.9)
```

Or, you could use one of the activate commands so you can avoid including the entire path:

```
$ source my-virtual-env/bin/activate
(my-virtual-env) $ python -m pip --version
pip 20.2.3 from /home/monty/code/my-virtual-env/lib/python3.9/site-packa
ges/pip (python 3.9)
```

This condensed style—where python points to a virtual environment Python binary—is the style that will be used through the rest of this chapter in our pip examples. Now that you've seen how to install pip packages in an isolated virtual environment, let's try it out.

Installing a Package with pip

Third-party packages installed via pip are essential to almost any significant Python codebase you might work on. If a teammate suggests you run a python3 -m pip install <some-string> command, it's because they want your program to have access to a third-party module that does something useful.

Installing a package with pip can be done using its install command:

```
❰ python3 -m pip install backports.zoneinfo==0.2.1
```

If you run this command you'll have installed version 0.2.1 of a package named backports.zoneinfo. backports.zoneinfo is a Python package with timezone information that you might have used in Writing Functions for Handling Timezones, on page 95.

At this point you could use backports.zoneinfo in a Python program. In the following example, we use the ZoneInfo class provided by backport.zoneinfo to represent the America/Los_Angeles timezone:

```
>>> from backports.zoneinfo import ZoneInfo
>>> la_timezone = ZoneInfo("America/Los_Angeles")
>>> print(str(la_timezone))
```

If you run those three lines in a Python interpreter, you should see output like the following:

```
❰ America/Los_Angeles
```

Additonal Requirement on Windows

To run the three lines from the example on Windows, you will also need to install the first-party pip package tzdata by running python3 -m pip install tzdata==2020.4.[1] This is because Windows, unlike other operating systems, does not include IANA timezone information by default.

You've now successfully used pip to install a commonly used package backports.tzinfo. In the next section we'll explore some of the risks associated with installing third-party packages.

Encountering Danger with pip

pip is usually safe, but it can be dangerous. Don't actually run this, but consider, for example, if a teammate advised you to run the following to install a package:

```
python3 -m pip install setup-tools
```

Your teammate assures you that this pip install is needed so you can run import setuptools in your code. (If you do not know what setuptools is, that's OK. All we need to understand is that setup-tools is an example of a third-party package we might want to install.)

Unfortunately, however, if you were to run the command you would you have just been subject to a "typosquatting" attack. The software you downloaded would not be the actual setuptools package, but a malicious variant that could be financially or personally destructive.

The pip package your co-worker probably meant to point you to is named setuptools. setup-tools, by contrast, is a malicious variant created by someone hoping that people might accidentally install their similarly named package instead of the real one.

2017 Typosquatting Attack

The setup-tools pip package was a real-life typosquatting package that existed in 2017. The malicious setup-tools was masquerading as the legitimate package setuptools. The malicious package was relatively benign and just collected hostnames from victim computers and uploaded them to a remote server. It would have been trivial, however, for the package to collect and exfiltrate much more sensitive information. setup-tools is no longer available for download via pip.

---

1. https://pypi.org/project/tzdata/

Using pip Safely

You've seen that running pip install commands can be dangerous if you aren't careful. If your teammate proposes that you run a python3 -m pip install <some-string> command, you should exercise caution.

Let's review two basic steps you can take use pip safely:

1. Verify that the pip install <package> command your teammate recommends actually matches the installation command stated in the package's online documentation.

2. Choose a specific version of the package to install: backports.zoneinfo==0.2.1 versus a bare backports.zoneinfo.

You can use these two steps as a first-pass sanity check on a package you are about to install.

Using pip Safely: Increased Specificity

It's possible to go a few steps further and gain additional confidence in a package you are about to install. In particular, you want to verify that the package you are downloading has the expected contents and that those contents don't unexpectedly change under you over time. For example, to install backports.zoneinfo, especially safely, we could create a file requirements.txt with a line that specifies the backports.zoneinfo package:

```
requirements.txt
backports.zoneinfo==0.2.1 \
--hash=sha256:\
fadbfe37f74051d024037f223b8e001611eac868b5c5b06144ef4d8b799862f2
```

Here, we've pinned backports.zoneinfo to a specific version (0.2.1) and also to a specific set of code as specified by the sha256 hash value. (The contents of requirements.txt is split into three lines using \ characters so that the lines fit within the margin of this book. Ordinarily, the \ characters can be deleted and the elements can just live on the same line.)

You can ask pip to ensure that it only installs backports.zoneinfo if it finds that specific version with that specific sha256 hash by using its -r and --require-hashes options:

```
python3 -m pip install -r requirements.txt --require-hashes
```

The -r in the command means "requirements" and it installs every line in the given file (in this case from requirements.txt) as a package (in our case, we only

What Is the sha256 Hash Value?

A sha256 hash is essentially a computed summary of all the contents in a file. If (and only if) two files have exactly the same contents, will two files share the exact same sha256 hash value. So, if a package author publishes a sha256 hash value for their project, they are effectively saying that, "the files in my package collectively have this sha256 hash value, otherwise you don't have my package." If this doesn't make complete sense, that's OK. The key to understand is that a sha256 hash value lets us check whether or not a set of files contains the exact contents we expect them to.

have one line with the backports.zoneinfo package). The --require-hashes option means that pip will ensure the packages it downloads have the contents we expect.

If you run the previous command, you'll see output like:

```
Collecting backports.zoneinfo==0.2.1
  Downloading backports.zoneinfo-0.2.1.tar.gz (74 kB)
     |████████████████████████████| 74 kB 1.5 MB/s
...etc...
Installing collected packages: backports.zoneinfo
Successfully installed backports.zoneinfo-0.2.1
```

pip successfully installed backports.zoneinfo after verifying the sha256 hash matched the value specified in the requirements.txt file.

Package Hashes May Be Operating System Dependent

The previous example specifies a sha256 hash specific to Python 3.9 linux distributions and may not work on your machine as written. Since Python package maintainers may publish slightly different code when they target different operating systems, the sha256 hashes may differ on different operating systems. To accommodate this, requirements.txt files can include multiple --hash=sha256:this-is-the-hash-value flags on each line (one for each targeted operating system, for example). For example: backports.zoneinfo==0.2.1 --hash=sha256:hash-for-OS-1 --hash=sha256:hash-for-OS-2

How do you find sha256 hash values to put in requirements.txt?

- Look for a sha256 hash independently published by the project's authors.

    - Not all packages owners independently publish these hashes, and unfortunately the backports.zoneinfo authors do not.

– As a contrasting example, the Django web framework package authors publish sha256 hashes independently.[2]

• If you cannot find a sha256 hash independently published by the authors, locate the package on the PyPI website,[3] and then find package checksums in the Download Files menu—for example, the package checksums link for backports.tzinfo.[4]

In this section you have learned about the potentially destructive power of pip and how to run pip safely. If a teammate suggests you install a package or add an entry to an existing requirements.txt file, you can sanity check the install and explicitly specify it with a sha256 hash.

Now that you have a good understanding of pip and its capabilities, it's worth mentioning some additional tools in the Python ecosystem for managing third-party packages.

Picking Other Tools For Managing Third-Party Python Packages

Many Python projects often depend on one more third-party packages.

There are a number of alternatives for specifying a project's dependencies on third-party packages. A common strategy—that we explored in the previous section—is to write a file named requirements.txt with a series of lines each indicating a different dependent package. python3 -m pip install -r requirements.txt (potentially also with the --require-hashes flag) is then used to install all the packages into a virtual environment previously created using the venv module. The requirements.txt strategy with the venv module is one of the simpler strategies for managing packages and is commonly used.

Several other strategies and tools for managing packages exist. Here are a few of them:

• pipenv[5]
• poetry[6]
• The anaconda Python distribution and its conda package manager.[7]
• Docker[8]

2. https://media.djangoproject.com/pgp/Django-2.2.checksum.txt
3. https://pypi.org/
4. https://pypi.org/project/backports.zoneinfo/0.2.1/#files
5. https://pipenv.pypa.io/en/latest/
6. https://python-poetry.org
7. https://www.anaconda.com
8. https://docs.docker.com/get-docker/

pipenv and poetry operate by providing high-level convenience interfaces over pip and venv. pipenv and poetry generally extend pip and venv to make them easier to use and more well suited to managing lists of dependent packages. The anaconda Python distribution and its conda package manager, by contrast, is an entirely separate Python distribution and package manager that is especially popular with scientists.

Different projects and teammates will be better served by different management solutions—pipenv, poetry, and anaconda can all serve you well. My first choice, however, is to use Docker to manage both my Python version and my third-party package dependencies. Docker gives you strong reproducibility and consistency between teammates: you'll all be running with same operating system, Python version, and set of installed dependencies. Additionally, the importance of maintaining many segmented virtual environments (using venv or some other tool) becomes less important with Docker—the Docker image is your isolation and you do not need to worry about cluttering or corrupting your host machine with Python + pip package installs.

You can look at the GitHub repository for this book's companion Docker image an example of a Docker-based approach to distributing and maintaining a reproducible runtime.[9] As you might expect, you can combine the Docker approach with another package manager like poetry. I try to stick to a simple pip + requirements.txt approach until it becomes overly cumbersome (for example, managing lots of packages and interrelated subdependencies that are being updated frequently).

You have covered a lot of ground with Python and third-party packages: you know how to use pip and venv, understand some dangers inherent to pip, and are aware of other tools that can help you manage your third-party packages. In the next section we'll move back to Python code and discuss Python's lack of variable privacy.

Maintaining Privacy in a Public World

Sometimes Python can feel like a bit of the wild wild west—this can feel especially true for programmers coming from a language like Java where variables and classes can be explicitly scoped as public, private, protected, and so on. In this section, you'll learn more about how variable privacy works in Python so you better understand how to protect your programs from unexpected manipulation.

---

9. https://github.com/DavidMuller/intuitive-python-book

Finding No Privacy in Python

Python programs do not support truly private variables, methods, or functions. Anything you define in a Python file can be discovered and potentially mangled by other parts of your program.

Let's consider an example class representing a dinosaur egg that can hatch:

```
dinosaur_egg.py
class DinosaurEgg:
    def __init__(self, egg_id):
        self.egg_id = egg_id
        self.hatch_status = None

    def hatch(self):
        if self.hatch_status is not None:
            raise ValueError(f"Egg {self.egg_id} has already been hatched.")
        self.hatch_status = "hatched"
        print(f"Egg {self.egg_id} has been successfully hatched.")
```

The example defines the DinosaurEgg class with one method named hatch. The hatch method raises a ValueError if a DinosaurEgg instance calls the hatch method more than once:

```
egg = DinosaurEgg(egg_id="raptor-1")
egg.hatch()
egg.hatch()  # hatch()'ing a second time will raise an error
```

If you load the DinosaurEgg class into an interpreter and run this code, you'll see output like the following:

```
Egg raptor-1 has been successfully hatched.
Traceback (most recent call last):
  File "dinosaur_egg.py", line 15, in <module>
    egg.hatch()  # hatch()'ing a second time will raise an error
  File "dinosaur_egg.py", line 8, in hatch
    raise ValueError(f"Egg {self.egg_id} has already been hatched.")
ValueError: Egg raptor-1 has already been hatched.
```

The first line of the output is the successful hatching of the 'raptor-1' egg. Since DinosaurEgg guards against an egg being hatched more than once, the remaining lines of the output are a ValueError Exception raised by the second call to hatch().

The DinosaurEgg class doesn't necessarily contain any bugs, but it's more permissive than it should be. Anyone using the DinosaurEgg can clobber the value of hatch_status and replace it with something else.

Continuing on with the preceding DinosaurEgg class, you can see how someone could manipulate hatch_status to suit their own needs:

```
t_rex_egg = DinosaurEgg(egg_id="t_rex-3")
for _ in range(3):
    t_rex_egg.hatch()
    t_rex_egg.hatch_status = None
```

This code defines a for loop that calls hatch on t_rex_egg and sets the value of t_rex_egg.hatch_status back to None. If you run the code, you'll see output like the following:

```
Egg t_rex-3 has been successfully hatched.
Egg t_rex-3 has been successfully hatched.
Egg t_rex-3 has been successfully hatched.
```

The code creating t_rex_egg continually overwrites the value of hatch_status to None so that it can hatch the t_rex-3 egg over and over again. Hatching an egg multiple times does not really make sense. It's also clear from DinosaurEgg's implementation that the original author did not intend for an egg to be hatched multiple times.

In other languages like Java, you might be able to declare a variable as private so that it wouldn't be made available to external users of a class. Python does not support private variables, but has a convention that programmers are encouraged to follow instead. We'll explore this convention next.

Indicate Privacy with an Underscore Prefix

You can improve DinosaurEgg by more clearly indicating that hatch_status is for internal use. Let's change self.hatch_status to self._hatch_status so as to discourage devious DinosaurEgg users from hatching an egg more than one time. The DinosaurEgg class can be updated to opt into the leading underscore privacy prefix:

dinosaur_egg_2.py
```
class DinosaurEgg:
    def __init__(self, egg_id):
        self.egg_id = egg_id
        self._hatch_status = None

    def hatch(self):
        if self._hatch_status is not None:
            raise ValueError(
                f"Egg {self.egg_id} has already been hatched."
            )
        self._hatch_status = "hatched"
        print(f"Egg {self.egg_id} has been successfully hatched.")
```

In this example self.hatch_status has been renamed to self._hatch_status. Unfortunately, it's true that nothing prevents DinosaurEgg users from updating the underscore-prefixed _hatch_status variable in the same way they could update hatch_status. The leading underscore, however, is an established Python convention for indicating privacy. Variables prefixed with _ pervade the stdlib and third-party packages.

Using namedtuple to Create Tamper Resistant Objects

As you learned in Preventing Field Reassignments with namedtuple, on page 41, namedtuple from the collections module can help you define objects that protect themselves from attribute reassignment. If you have an object without much mutable state (perhaps a CSV row or configuration data), consider reaching for namedtuple to build a compact, tamper resistant, and easy to debug object.

You've learned that a leading underscore makes it clear that _hatch_status is a private attribute that shouldn't be manipulated. In the next section we'll explore another danger common to Python projects: keeping files organized.

Keeping Your Source Organized

Just like the dinosaurs in *Jurassic Park*, Python codebases have a habit of breaking out from inside the fenced pens we try to create for them. One particularly vexing problem can be keeping project code organized. As time passes, code starts to live in places it shouldn't and it can become increasingly difficult to find what files code should live in or where new code should be placed. In this section, we'll explore a general strategy that uses Python's built-in unittest module to keep a directory organized.

Maintaining Organization in a tests/ Directory

Many Python codebases contain tests to help verify that they are working correctly. Frequently, these tests are defined in a directory named tests/ at the top level of the codebase. The tests/ directory structure typically matches the directory structure in the corresponding source directory that is being tested.

Let's consider a Python project with the following directory structure:

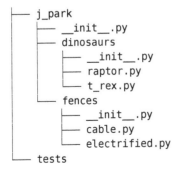

```
├── j_park
│   ├── __init__.py
│   ├── dinosaurs
│   │   ├── __init__.py
│   │   ├── raptor.py
│   │   └── t_rex.py
│   └── fences
│       ├── __init__.py
│       ├── cable.py
│       └── electrified.py
└── tests
```

```
    ├── __init__.py
    ├── fences
    │   ├── __init__.py
    │   └── test_cable.py
    ├── test_electrified.py
    └── test_raptor.py
```

This source tree has a j_park/ directory with source code and a tests/ directory with test_*.py files that correspond to source files in j_park/.

If you look at this tree, you'll see that the layout of the j_park/ directory has diverged from the layout in tests/. Among other inconsistencies, test_electrified.py is at the root level of tests/ instead of in the tests/fences/ subdirectory. Additionally, test_raptor.py is orphaned at the root level of tests/ instead of occupying a place in a tests/dinosaurs/ subdirectory.

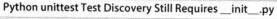

Python unittest Test Discovery Still Requires __init__.py

In Python 3, you generally do not need to create __init__.py files like you did in Python 2. The __init__.py files are included in this example, however, because a longstanding bug prevents Python unittest discovery (for example, python3 -m unittest discover --help) from finding test files that don't have __init__.py siblings.[10]

With the existing disorganization, it would be unsurprising to receive a change request that updates the directory layout so that jurassic_park/ and tests/ diverge further:

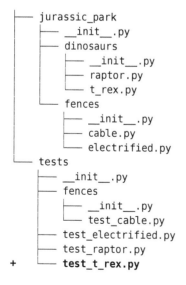

```
├── jurassic_park
│   ├── __init__.py
│   ├── dinosaurs
│   │   ├── __init__.py
│   │   ├── raptor.py
│   │   └── t_rex.py
│   └── fences
│       ├── __init__.py
│       ├── cable.py
│       └── electrified.py
└── tests
    ├── __init__.py
    ├── fences
    │   ├── __init__.py
    │   └── test_cable.py
    ├── test_electrified.py
    ├── test_raptor.py
+   └── test_t_rex.py
```

---

10. https://stackoverflow.com/a/53976736

Notice in the example that a new file test_t_rex.py has been added directly under tests/. This doesn't match j_park/ where t_rex.py lives under the dinosaurs/ subdirectory.

The tests/ directory is becoming increasingly divergent from the j_park/ source directory. As the project accumulates more files, it becomes harder and harder to find where a source code is tested. It's true that this disorganization may not be the end of the world, but it increases the barrier to entry to your project. Where does test code live? Where should new contributors find tests? How do they know if something is already tested? You notice this and may feel a bit wary—let's address this wariness and capitalize on the opportunity to improve the code's organization.

You can mandate that the j_park/ and tests/ directory layouts match using a unittest TestCase in a new file tests/test_directory_layout.py:

```
test_directory_layout.py
import unittest
from pathlib import Path


class TestDirectoryLayout(unittest.TestCase):
    def test_tests_layout_matches_j_park(self):
        # verify that this file is - itself - in tests/
        this_files_path = Path(__file__)
        tests_dir = this_files_path.parent
        self.assertEqual(tests_dir.name, "tests")

        # get a path to the j_park/ source directory
        j_park_path = Path(tests_dir.parent, "j_park")

        # loop through all test_*.py files in tests/
        # (and its subdirectories)
        for test_file_path in tests_dir.glob("**/test_*.py"):
            # skip this file: we don't expect there to be a
            # corresponding source file for this layout enforcer
            if test_file_path == this_files_path:
                continue

            # construct the expected source_path
            source_rel_dir = test_file_path.relative_to(tests_dir).parent
            source_name = test_file_path.name.split("test_", maxsplit=1)[1]
            source_path = Path(j_park_path, source_rel_dir, source_name)

            error_msg = (
                f"{test_file_path} found, but {source_path} missing."
            )
            self.assertTrue(source_path.is_file(), msg=error_msg)
```

The TestCase class TestDirectoryLayout defines a single test method named test_tests_layout_matches_j_park. Using the pathlib standard library module, the test method loops through every test_*.py in the tests/ directory and ensures that the test_*.py file corresponds to a source file. If some of the functions used in the test shown look unfamiliar, that's OK. The most important thing to keep in mind is the strategy of writing a test case that forces you and your team-mates to follow a pattern and stay organized—that you keep holes out of your fences. I encourage you to adapt the test into any of your own projects.

If you were to duplicate the preceding directory structure and run the test using the unittest module

```
python3 -m unittest tests/test_directory_layout.py
```

you might see a failure message like the following:

```
AssertionError: False is not true : /home/user/code/tests/test_raptor.py
  found, but /home/user/code/j_park/raptor.py missing.
```

The output indicates that test_raptor.py does not correspond to an actual source file: it is an orphan. You have successfully added a test that automatically detects when other tests are out of position and do not correspond to a source file.

If you repeatedly run the test—fixing the failure messages as you go—your tests/ directory will eventually match the layout of j_park/ and will be continually enforced. The eventual output of your corrections will look like the following:

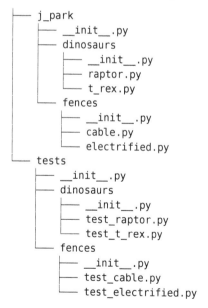

```
├── j_park
│   ├── __init__.py
│   ├── dinosaurs
│   │   ├── __init__.py
│   │   ├── raptor.py
│   │   └── t_rex.py
│   └── fences
│       ├── __init__.py
│       ├── cable.py
│       └── electrified.py
└── tests
    ├── __init__.py
    ├── dinosaurs
    │   ├── __init__.py
    │   ├── test_raptor.py
    │   └── test_t_rex.py
    └── fences
        ├── __init__.py
        ├── test_cable.py
        └── test_electrified.py
```

Think of other ways you can add unit tests that improve your day-to-day living experience in a code base. It might be useful to, for example, write a unit test that enforces any configuration files, CSV files, and so on in your code base to store their contents in alphabetical order. Having their contents in order makes the files more pleasant to read and edit. Anytime you catch yourself writing a comment like # Please keep this list in alphabetical order, consider using Python's high level tooling to write a test that mandates the constraint instead.

In the final section of this chapter, we'll explore a risk a little more direct than disorganized file systems: wildcard variable shadowing.

Dodging Wildcard Variable Shadowing

Few things are more destructive for a code base then a programmer operating under flawed assumptions. We want to write code that makes it clear to others what calling a piece of code does and what effects it might have.

In an earlier chapter, you learned how to use flake8 to catch certain types of errors before you even run your Python code. One of the dangerous classes of errors that flake8 helps you avoid is variable shadowing from * ("wildcard") imports.

Consider the following toy file that provides two methods for managing dinosaurs:

```
dinosaur_manager.py
from veterinarian import *
from lab import *

def euthanize_dinosaurs():
    for dinosaur in get_dinosaurs():
        print(f"Euthanizing {dinosaur}")

def run_experiments():
    for dinosaur in get_dinosaurs():
        print(f"Running experiment on {dinosaur}")
```

The euthanize_dinosaurs function euthanizes all dinosaurs returned by get_dinosaurs. The run_experiments function runs an experiment on all dinosaurs returned by get_dinosaurs. But, where is get_dinosaurs defined? Is it defined in veterinarian or in lab? Is it defined in both?

For the sake of example, let's say both veterinarian and lab defined a get_dinosaurs function. Which dinosaurs would be euthanized? The ones from veterinarian or the ones from lab? Since from veterinarian import * comes first, and from lab import * comes after, Python will bind get_dinosaurs to the most recently imported version (the version from lab).

Unfortunately, this means that calling euthanize_dinosaurs would euthanize all the dinosaurs in the lab instead of the terminally ill ones currently at the veterinarian.

This example might feel a bit contrived, but now you know how dangerous variable shadowing can be—it could cost a dinosaur its life! flake8 forbids wildcard (*) imports to help you avoid just these sorts of situations.

Let's consider how we could rewrite dinosaur_manager.py so its intentions are clear by removing * imports:

dinosaur_manager_2.py
```
from veterinarian import get_dinosaurs as get_dinosaurs_at_vet
from lab import get_dinosaurs as get_dinosaurs_at_lab

def euthanize_dinosaurs():
    for dinosaur in get_dinosaurs_at_vet():
        print(f"Euthanizing {dinosaur}")

def run_experiments():
    for dinosaur in get_dinosaurs_at_lab():
        print(f"Running experiment on {dinosaur}")
```

Our new file dinosaur_manager_2.py is unambiguous. Dinosaurs at the veterinarian are euthanized. Dinosaurs in the lab are subjects for experimentation and are not euthanized.

Wildcard * imports pervade a lot of open source code and many projects. While sometimes convenient as a shorthand, you've learned how * imports significantly risk the correctness of your program and should be avoided.

Wrapping Up

In this chapter we have discussed different strategies for hardening your code. In particular, you have learned how to install third-party pip packages securely, how to privatize variables in Python, how to keep a directory of tests/ organized, and the dangers of wildcard imports. You can use these lessons to improve your code base's organization and help avoid dangerous classes of unexpected bugs.

No island will ever be built rigorously enough to contain all its dinosaurs, but you can always improve your system just a little bit more to make it resilient to life's efforts to free itself.

You've reached the end of this book, but only the beginning of your possible experience with Python. You've covered a lot of ground already. In the beginning of this book, you explored Python's interpreted nature and learned techniques for improving your code with static analysis tools like flake8. You moved on to touring some of the finer parts of the standard library including the collections module and tempfile. As the book progressed, you built meta-level understanding of Python projects including how to harness concurrent code and the inherent dangers of pickle and pip.

I've been writing Python for my entire adult life, and I still find myself learning new patterns, discovering new tools, yelling in frustration at some inane bug, and experiencing an intoxicating high after fixing that bug. I hope you can experience the same.

Thank you!

How did you enjoy this book? Please let us know. Take a moment and email us at support@pragprog.com with your feedback. Tell us your story and you could win free ebooks. Please use the subject line "Book Feedback."

Ready for your next great Pragmatic Bookshelf book? Come on over to https://pragprog.com and use the coupon code BUYANOTHER2021 to save 30% on your next ebook.

Void where prohibited, restricted, or otherwise unwelcome. Do not use ebooks near water. If rash persists, see a doctor. Doesn't apply to *The Pragmatic Programmer* ebook because it's older than the Pragmatic Bookshelf itself. Side effects may include increased knowledge and skill, increased marketability, and deep satisfaction. Increase dosage regularly.

And thank you for your continued support,

The Pragmatic Bookshelf

Modern CSS with Tailwind

Tailwind CSS is an exciting new CSS framework that allows you to design your site by composing simple utility classes to create complex effects. With Tailwind, you can style your text, move your items on the page, design complex page layouts, and adapt your design for devices from a phone to a wide-screen monitor. With this book, you'll learn how to use the Tailwind for its flexibility and its consistency, from the smallest detail of your typography to the entire design of your site.

Noel Rappin
(90 pages) ISBN: 9781680508185. $26.95
https://pragprog.com/book/tailwind

Resourceful Code Reuse

Reusing well-written, well-debugged, and well-tested code improves productivity, code quality, and software configurability and relieves pressure on software developers. When you organize your code into self-contained modular units, you can use them as building blocks for your future projects and share them with other programmers, if needed. Understand the benefits and downsides of seven code reuse models so you can confidently reuse code at any development stage. Create static and dynamic libraries in C and Python, two of the most popular modern programming languages. Adapt your code for the real world: deploy shared functions remotely and build software that accesses them using remote procedure calls.

Dmitry Zinoviev
(64 pages) ISBN: 9781680508208. $14.99
https://pragprog.com/book/dzreuse

Distributed Services with Go

This is the book for Gophers who want to learn how to build distributed systems. You know the basics of Go and are eager to put your knowledge to work. Build distributed services that are highly available, resilient, and scalable. This book is just what you need to apply Go to real-world situations. Level up your engineering skills today.

Travis Jeffery
(258 pages) ISBN: 9781680507607. $45.95
https://pragprog.com/book/tjgo

Explore Software Defined Radio

Do you want to be able to receive satellite images using nothing but your computer, an old TV antenna, and a $20 USB stick? Now you can. At last, the technology exists to turn your computer into a super radio receiver, capable of tuning in to FM, shortwave, amateur "ham," and even satellite frequencies, around the world and above it. Listen to police, fire, and aircraft signals, both in the clear and encoded. And with the book's advanced antenna design, there's no limit to the signals you can receive.

Wolfram Donat
(78 pages) ISBN: 9781680507591. $19.95
https://pragprog.com/book/wdradio

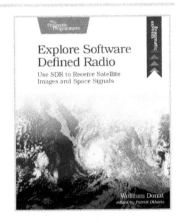

Genetic Algorithms in Elixir

From finance to artificial intelligence, genetic algorithms are a powerful tool with a wide array of applications. But you don't need an exotic new language or framework to get started; you can learn about genetic algorithms in a language you're already familiar with. Join us for an in-depth look at the algorithms, techniques, and methods that go into writing a genetic algorithm. From introductory problems to real-world applications, you'll learn the underlying principles of problem solving using genetic algorithms.

Sean Moriarity
(242 pages) ISBN: 9781680507942. $39.95
https://pragprog.com/book/smgaelixir

Design and Build Great Web APIs

APIs are transforming the business world at an increasing pace. Gain the essential skills needed to quickly design, build, and deploy quality web APIs that are robust, reliable, and resilient. Go from initial design through prototyping and implementation to deployment of mission-critical APIs for your organization. Test, secure, and deploy your API with confidence and avoid the "release into production" panic. Tackle just about any API challenge with more than a dozen open-source utilities and common programming patterns you can apply right away.

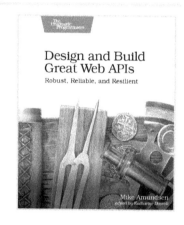

Mike Amundsen
(330 pages) ISBN: 9781680506808. $45.95
https://pragprog.com/book/maapis

Quantum Computing

You've heard that quantum computing is going to change the world. Now you can check it out for yourself. Learn how quantum computing works, and write programs that run on the IBM Q quantum computer, one of the world's first functioning quantum computers. Develop your intuition to apply quantum concepts for challenging computational tasks. Write programs to trigger quantum effects and speed up finding the right solution for your problem. Get your hands on the future of computing today.

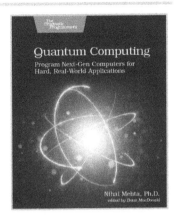

Nihal Mehta, Ph.D.
(580 pages) ISBN: 9781680507201. $45.95
https://pragprog.com/book/nmquantum

A Common-Sense Guide to Data Structures and Algorithms, Second Edition

If you thought that data structures and algorithms were all just theory, you're missing out on what they can do for your code. Learn to use Big O notation to make your code run faster by orders of magnitude. Choose from data structures such as hash tables, trees, and graphs to increase your code's efficiency exponentially. With simple language and clear diagrams, this book makes this complex topic accessible, no matter your background. This new edition features practice exercises in every chapter, and new chapters on topics such as dynamic programming and heaps and tries. Get the hands-on info you need to master data structures and algorithms for your day-to-day work.

Jay Wengrow
(506 pages) ISBN: 9781680507225. $45.95
https://pragprog.com/book/jwdsal2

The Pragmatic Bookshelf

The Pragmatic Bookshelf features books written by professional developers for professional developers. The titles continue the well-known Pragmatic Programmer style and continue to garner awards and rave reviews. As development gets more and more difficult, the Pragmatic Programmers will be there with more titles and products to help you stay on top of your game.

Visit Us Online

This Book's Home Page
https://pragprog.com/book/dmpython
Source code from this book, errata, and other resources. Come give us feedback, too!

Keep Up to Date
https://pragprog.com
Join our announcement mailing list (low volume) or follow us on twitter @pragprog for new titles, sales, coupons, hot tips, and more.

New and Noteworthy
https://pragprog.com/news
Check out the latest pragmatic developments, new titles and other offerings.

Save on the ebook

Save on the ebook versions of this title. Owning the paper version of this book entitles you to purchase the electronic versions at a terrific discount.

PDFs are great for carrying around on your laptop—they are hyperlinked, have color, and are fully searchable. Most titles are also available for the iPhone and iPod touch, Amazon Kindle, and other popular e-book readers.

Send a copy of your receipt to support@pragprog.com and we'll provide you with a discount coupon.

Contact Us

Online Orders:	*https://pragprog.com/catalog*
Customer Service:	*support@pragprog.com*
International Rights:	*translations@pragprog.com*
Academic Use:	*academic@pragprog.com*
Write for Us:	*http://write-for-us.pragprog.com*
Or Call:	+1 800-699-7764